EBONY and SPICA

Two Birds in My Life

by Janet Doolaege

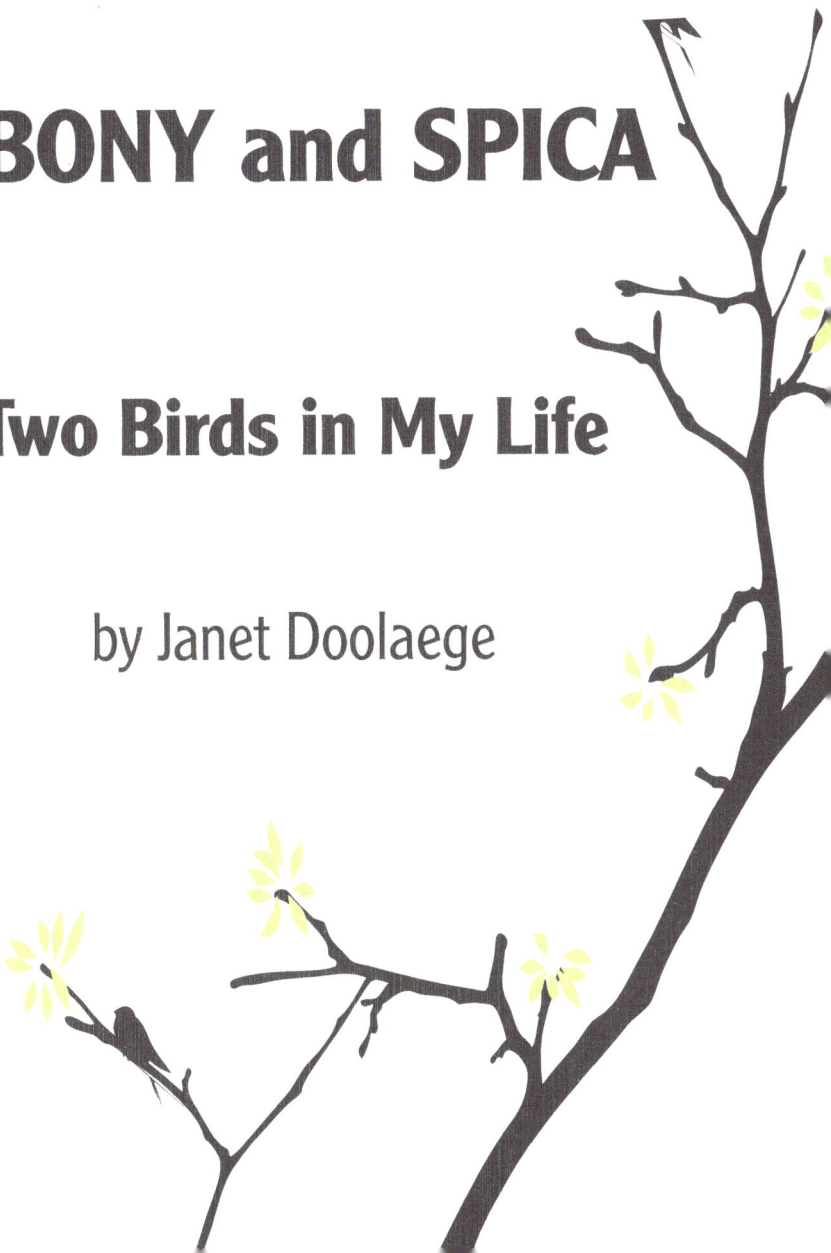

Published by New Generation Publishing in 2014

Copyright © Janet Doolaege 2014

First Print Edition

Cover design: © Alain Perry
Illustrations: © Carol Jean Watkins and © Alain Perry
Photos: p.53 © Howard Klaaste
p.77 © Steven Ryland
p.80 © anat chant
p.86 © xpixel
Vector images: © Shutterstock
Interior design: Marianne Weeks

www.newgeneration-publishing.com

New Generation Publishing

To Lloyd and Rose Buck

This is a true story.

with best wishes from
a bird-lover

Janet Doolaege

PART ONE

EBONY

BRINGING UP A BLACKBIRD

A tremendous commotion broke out in the garden nine floors below my Paris flat: screeching and a chorus of staccato alarm calls. From the balcony I could see a pair of blackbirds that seemed to be dive-bombing a shrub. Then I caught a glimpse of black and white fur. One of the several cats that used the garden for caterwauling in the evenings must have caught a bird. I rushed out of the flat and trundled slowly downwards in the lift, hoping that I wouldn't be too late.

I think I may have been a bird myself in a former life. Somehow, birds have kept cropping up. As a small child, I was fascinated by my father's German cuckoo-clock, and then distressed by the pathetic dead baby sparrows that our cat, Timmy, used to bring into the house. Later, growing up in Dorset, I learned to recognize songs and plumage, chaffinch, bullfinch, wren and goldcrest, and on long country walks with my friend Chris we would look for nests, scrambling up into hedges to feel the warm eggs, but taking care not to leave the nest exposed. We had shouting matches with boys who were intent on stealing eggs for their collections. We sat in trees and watched parent birds

coming and going with nesting materials and beakfuls of food for the nestlings. We kept anxious watch as fledglings left their nests, and neighbours' cats were driven off with streams of water from old washing-up liquid bottles. We did what we could to protect these fragile yet tough, elusive and attractive creatures, flitting around so close to us in our gardens and parks.

When I moved to France and found myself living in a flat rather than a house, I missed the company of birds, and went to look at canaries, budgerigars and more exotic specimens for sale every Sunday morning at the Bird Market on the Ile de la Cité, near Notre Dame. I remembered my aunt's blue budgie, Lucky, who used to recite bits of nursery rhymes, interspersed with exclamations of "pretty boy!" and who used to perch on the end of her knitting-needle, bobbing up and down as she knitted. Of course, I couldn't resist buying some birds of my own to take care of. It made such a difference at the end of a working day to come home to bright-eyed beings hopping about, singing and feeding, rather than to an empty flat. If these birds had been born in captivity, it didn't seem any more unkind to keep them in spacious cages than it would have been to keep, say, a cat in a flat. Nowadays, I would be more circumspect. Today, trade in exotic species has been strictly curbed, and rightly so. At the time, I believed that all those brilliantly coloured birds sold at the Bird Market had been born in captivity, but very probably some of the more beautiful ones had been caught in the wild and imported, together with many others that did not survive the journey.

There are few good reasons for taking a wild bird from its natural environment. But what about a very young, injured wild bird?

In the garden surrounded on three sides by blocks of flats, the blackbirds were still scolding shrilly and the cat slunk into view. I ran at it, arms whirling, shouting, and after one startled glance it scampered off. I peered under the shrub.

"It's under the other one," said a voice above my head, and looking up I saw a neighbour on her second-floor balcony. "The cat caught it but it escaped and went under that shrub."

Sure enough, under a laurel skulked a young blackbird, speckled brown and with only a stump of a tail. He was at the age when young birds hop after their parents, begging, as they

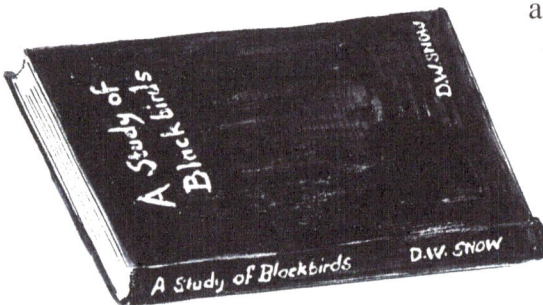

search for food on lawns. They are particularly vulnerable to predators at this stage, as their reactions are slow and they draw attention to themselves by calling loudly and fluttering their wings. He tried to avoid me as I went to pick him up, but it wasn't difficult to catch him. Holding one hand over his wings to stop him struggling, I examined him. There was blood on his back, and one eye was gashed. The other eye was the beautiful black liquid orb common to all blackbirds, and his beak still had the yellow hinges of babyhood. As I held him, soft and warm, he opened his beak and gave the loud, sweet begging call that is almost impossible to ignore.

Where had the cat gone? What was I going to do with him? He was hurt, and if I left him there, the cat would soon return and finish him off.

I took him back up to my flat.

In the kitchen, I inspected him. His injuries didn't appear to be too serious. I bathed his back as well as I could through the feathers, and although he had blood in his right eye, he could apparently still see with it. One wing drooped slightly, and his right foot was a little deformed, with

the "thumb" twisted forwards instead of backwards for gripping branches. I didn't think that the cat had hurt his foot. It could have been crushed in the nest by his heavier brothers and sisters, or perhaps he had hatched like that. As soon as I had put him in a cardboard box, he squatted there trustingly, his large feet splayed, and demanded to be fed. He seemed not much the worse for his ordeal, and not at all afraid of me.

I was going to have to feed him, at any rate.

Most of my available wall space consisted of bookcases. Now that I had a full-time job as a translator, I hated to part with any of my books from the past. Luckily I remembered one that described what to do with rescued birds, and having consulted it I made a sort of paste with crumbled biscottes and water. (Later, on the vet's advice, I would add yolk of hard-boiled egg to this mixture and some raw mincemeat.) I tried offering the little bird some of this on the end of a small tool from a manicure set which I had already used in the past to feed rescued baby sparrows. His enthusiastic response was immediate. Opening his beak wide to display the orange-pink interior, he gave urgent begging calls and shivered his wings as I thrust the food into his gullet.

"Now whatever am I going to do with you?" I asked him in English. I already talked to my other birds quite naturally in French, but for some reason I found myself speaking English to this one.

He didn't seem able to fly, though clearly he must have flown or glided out of the nest, and his drooping wing made me wonder whether he had strained it in his struggle with the cat. Although he could see movements with his damaged eye, he always turned his head and used his left eye when he wanted to examine anything closely. He was certainly slightly disabled, and it didn't seem likely that he would survive for long if I just let him go. But how could I manage? I had to work during office hours, and couldn't be at home all the time to take care of him.

He soon started trying to jump out of his box, so I decided to let him loose in the dining room, where my other birds already lived in cages. He hopped around the parquet floor, exploring. When he had disappeared into the darkest and farthest corner underneath a piece of furniture, he would stop, open his beak and make a piercing demand for food. I would have to follow him around and then, on all fours, try to feed him.

This wouldn't do. Down in the cellar I knew I had a small cage with a door in the top, originally bought for a chipmunk that I had once owned who had later graduated to a bigger cage. This blackbird would have to be kept in the cage for feeding

purposes, although he could be let out for exercise.

The arrangement worked quite well for a time. I would feed him several times in the morning, then go to work, hurry home by métro in the lunch-hour and feed him again, then resume feeding in the evenings. Luckily he was not a featherless nestling, or he would have needed more frequent feeds. As it was, I was kept quite busy. There could be no sauntering around shops in the lunch hour, or enjoying anything longer than a hasty bite in the cafeteria. It was fortunate that the office was not more than half an hour away, door to door, but I admit that my lunch hours were stretched a bit in those early days.

Almost at once, he started preening his brown juvenile feathers, but one day he began to roll violently around the cage. "Whatever's wrong?" I was about to open the cage when I realized that he had got his beak stuck in the scab that had formed on his back. I thought that I would have to help him, but suddenly he broke free and crouched looking bemused for a while. Eventually the wound healed without trace.

My more exotic birds took no notice of him whatsoever, nor he of them.

After a time, he began to try to get out of the small cage, too. Blackbirds need space. He would jump up, cling to the bars and fall back down again. One day, when my friend Sue had come to stay and I was out shopping, he jumped up and somehow got his claws stuck in the bars.

"I found him hanging upside down. His head was drooping and his eyes were starting to close," she told me with concern. "I managed to unhook him. Do you think he's all right?"

"Oh, thank you! If you hadn't been there, he would probably have given up and died. You saved his life!"

But it was clear that I would have to find a more suitable cage.

Down I went to the cellar once more and brought up the larger cage that had also housed my chipmunk. The chipmunk used to roam around the flat too, climbing nimbly up the bookcases and storing nuts behind the books. To this day, some of my books have nibbled edges to their pages. Anyway, I put several perches into the cage at various heights, but Ebony spent his time on the floor of the cage at first. Then, one day in September, my cleaner happened to make a clatter which startled him, and he flew up to the top perch and stayed there, looking rather surprised. The perches were a bit too thin for his large feet to grip, so my boss helpfully gave me a small branch from his garden. I wedged this into the cage and immediately it proved very popular.

I had started to call him Ebony because I expected that eventually he would be jet black. For the time being he was still brown and speckled, and there was no way of telling whether he was a male or a female until he grew his adult plumage. But I strongly suspected him of being a male, because he was so vocal. It's the males that sing, of course. Apart from his begging call, he would make little remarks to himself as he hopped around, and he and I would whistle to each other with an intonation like "cuckoo". Whenever I was at home, I let him out of his cage, and from hopping around on the parquet floor he progressed to flying up to chair-backs and then to the tops of bookcases. Nobody had to teach him to fly: it came quite naturally.

Time passed. Every day, after work, I would find Ebony waiting for me. He would whistle his two-note greeting, and I would let him out to hop and fly around the dining room. Much mopping of white splodges on the parquet floor needed to be done, but that was the price to be paid for living with a blackbird.

By now, to my relief, he had learned a great deal: to feed himself, drink water, wipe his beak, fly, scratch his head, stand on his good leg with the other curled up out of sight, and take baths that sent showers of water across the floor. In November he began to moult. Sure enough, as I had expected, his adult feathers came through shiny and black. His head was the last to change, and the spiny new feathers pushing through on the top of his head made him look, at first, rather like a hedgehog. His tail feathers had grown, his beak turned from brown to yellow, starting with the tip, and he was recognizably a male blackbird, with a fine gold ring around each large black eye: very stylish. Later, though, his moult was not always successful, and there were times when he looked untidy rather than sleek, and other times when the nape of his neck was actually bald. This may have been due to some deficiency in his diet, although I bought him packets of special food for insectivores and a constant supply of mealworms from the Bird Market on the Ile de la Cité. Exposure to electric light, rather than the natural cycle of daylight and darkness, can also cause moulting problems, I learned.

I was advised not to feed him earthworms (always supposing I could find any in Paris) as they might have given him parasites. I'm sure he would have eaten one if offered: in fact I once had to intervene hastily to stop him from swallowing a rubber band that he had presumably mistaken for an earthworm. On the vet's advice, he was given the crumbled yolk of a hard-boiled egg once a week, and he also enjoyed lettuce and apples. One day, when I had served some home-made ginger ice cream for my then partner, Michel, Ebony joined us, hopping on the table, and started to peck my hand until I removed it from the dish. Next, he perched on the rim and helped himself to ginger ice cream with every sign of enjoyment.

Probably because they tend to be omnivorous, blackbirds have thrived in towns and cities, whereas thrushes, which have a more specialized diet consisting largely of snails, have become rare.

He accepted me from the outset as the provider of food, and had no objection to hopping on to my wrist so that I could let him out of his cage. However, he didn't actively seek contact and would only very rarely perch on my shoulder. Blackbirds have quite a large personal space and dislike other creatures intruding into it. You can see the frontiers of this personal space being pushed to and fro as blackbirds skirmish in a garden. One will hop and run aggressively towards another, who will hurry away and then stop. Then the second one may hop, head lowered, towards the first, who in turn hops away. If they get too close, they will fly up in the air, fighting with beak and claws.

Ebony objected to people walking too close to his cage and would lean forward, opening his beak threateningly. Once, when some friends had come to dinner, one man was holding forth vehemently with expansive gestures. He never noticed that whenever his gesturing hand approached the cage, Ebony leaned forward with his beak fiercely agape. My friend was unaware that I was smiling, not at his fascinating discourse, but at Ebony's antics behind him. Now that this bird was an adult, he would also open his beak menacingly at me; this was a provocation, so one day I opened my mouth wide at him. The effect was immediate. He suddenly looked twice as aggressive while at the same time nimbly backing into a corner. Clearly, he knew that my face was a face, even though beaks and mouths are not very similar.

He wasn't always sure of what he was watching, however. He could spot a mealworm moving across the floor and would pounce on it. But several times I noticed him gazing very attentively out of the window with his good eye.

"Whatever are you peering at, little bird?"

I was puzzled. Then I realized that in the distance he could see the suburban trains going by. Moving regularly along, and apparently quite small, they did look very like worms.

He was also interested in shiny objects, and by persistent pecking he once dislodged a small coin that had got wedged under a radiator, unnoticed by me or my cleaner. Some things that he saw displeased him, however. He liked me to be soberly attired and not to wear anything gaudy or boldly patterned. I owned a dress that he disapproved of because it had a row of large buttons down the front, and he would lean forwards threateningly towards the buttons with his beak open.

Until now I had been renting a flat, but there were disadvantages. The rent increased regularly, and the layout was impractical if friends came to stay. I would sleep on the bed-settee in the living room, but this meant that the friends in the bedroom could not get into the kitchen in the night or early in the morning. Another problem was the presence of cockroaches. Although it was a modern block of flats, it was infested with the disgusting insects, apparently impervious to insecticide.

My aim had always been to buy my own place, and at last I had saved up enough to make a down payment. I found a flat that I liked, this time on the eleventh floor of a block in the 13th arrondissement. I would be moving – and would have to move my birds, including Ebony.

When the day came, a colleague very kindly helped me to transfer the cages in his car. None of the birds enjoyed the experience, and Ebony flapped about, losing his balance on his perch and giving his "Pop! Pop!" alarm call. Eventually they were all installed in the room set aside for them at one end of the flat, and all went well until the removal men came down the corridor carrying my large desk. Ebony was in such a panic that he burst out of one of the closed doors of his cage and flung himself at the window with a screech. If it had been open, all would have been lost, but luckily it was closed and he slid down to the floor. "Stop moving!" I called urgently to the burly men, and they put down the desk while I rescued him and returned him to his cage. I then fastened the openings with wire and threw a blanket over the entire cage so that he couldn't see any alarming events. He calmed down after that.

My own flat! The kitchen and living room looked out over the street, but the balcony was high enough to give me a glimpse of the Sacré Coeur far away to the right. The tiny guest room, fitted with bunk beds, had a small window from which one could actually see the Eiffel Tower. But the widest vista was to be seen from the "bird room" at the other end of the flat, looking east over miles of pitched roofs, chimney-pots, flat roofs of apartment blocks, and the featureless slabs of tower blocks over to the right, in the 13th arrondissement. From the window of this room I could watch great rain clouds looming on the horizon and gusting across the sky, and the changing light glittering on countless windows. Only one tree could be seen, a horse chestnut in the yard of an old building immediately below.

The birds and I gradually settled in, and eventually all my belongings were stowed away. Instead of lying in a colossal pile of cardboard boxes in the middle of the living room, my books were properly arranged in bookcases. I bought plants for the balcony.

Now there was a new room for Ebony to explore when I let him out for exercise. I had taken the precaution of having vinyl floor tiles put down in the bird room, instead of carpet or parquet, as it was impossible to stop him making a mess on the floor. But he loved to be let out, and particularly enjoyed taking a vigorous bath in the middle of the floor, provided that I was not in the room. He didn't like

to be watched while bathing (well, who does?), probably because birds are more vulnerable when their feathers are waterlogged. But sometimes I would watch him through the keyhole. He would change from a sleek, plump bird to a thin, scruffy ragamuffin, his feathers all plastered to his body untidily until a vigorous preening session restored his appearance. What a mess he made, too: bath water, droppings and insectivore food all mixed together on the floor, to be cleared up by me once he had been put back in his cage. He seemed to enjoy hearing me say "What a mess!" as I mopped and swept, and he would make little contented noises, sinking down on his perch so that his feet disappeared under his fluffed-out feathers.

He wasn't always ready to go back in, however. He knew very well what I meant when I said "Time to go back in your cage," and would fly to the top of the bureau-bookcase. I would climb on to a chair and offer him my wrist. Then he would fly across the room to the top of another bookcase. I would step off the chair, follow him, climb on to another chair and hold out my wrist again. He would fly back to the bureau-bookcase. This workout could go on for a quarter of an hour until we were both panting with the effort. Then at last he would hop on to my wrist, I would take him back to his cage, and he would hop into it quite willingly, as his tasty supper of mealworms would be waiting for him.

No doubt the exercise was doing us both good, I would console myself ruefully as the two of us caught our breath.

My previous cleaner had left and I hadn't found another. Evenings and weekends were so precious that I didn't relish the prospect of doing all the housework myself. At this point, Robert began to take over the chores, and to take care of the birds, too, when necessary. Robert is, to say the least, unconventional, and he had only a part-time, poorly paid job. The arrangement suited both of us.

One day, I noticed that Ebony was sitting hunched on his perch and looking rather morose. He hadn't even eaten his full morning ration of worms. As I watched, he scratched the side of his neck vigorously, and little drops of blood flew about. What was wrong? I took him, protesting, in my hands to examine him, and found a nasty gash on the side of his neck. I didn't know how he had managed to hurt himself, but apparently he had done it with the claw on his deformed right foot. He returned to his miserable posture in his cage. Clearly, he was going to need professional help.

As luck would have it, I had made a note of the address and phone number of one of the very few vets in Paris who undertook to treat sick birds, for birds are much more delicate and difficult to deal with than the usual dogs and cats. I lost no time in phoning for an appointment. Then, as it was a working day, I had to explain to my boss that

I needed some time off to take a sick blackbird to the vet. Luckily he had been interested in hearing about Ebony's progress and was more understanding than many a boss might have been. Ebony was transferred to a smaller cage for transport, the cage was put into a bag in the hope that he wouldn't be frightened by all the changes and movement around him, and we set off. I travelled with him on the métro, wondering anxiously how he would cope with the roaring din of the trains.

"It's a good thing you brought him to me," said the vet. "That's a nasty gash. He would have continued to scratch it, it wouldn't have healed, and he would have just given up. He would have stopped eating and died."

"What can you do for him?" I asked urgently.

"I'll have to keep him overnight, anaesthetize him and stitch up the wound."

Oh dear. Such a major intervention for such a small being.

I left him there, all alone in his small cage, in the unfamiliar surroundings of the vet's surgery. Would he be all right? How would he react to the anaesthetic? Back at the flat, his large cage was silent and empty. I kept looking at it and missing him.

The next day in the office I found it difficult to concentrate on my work. What was happening to Ebony? In the afternoon, as agreed once again with my kind boss, I took the métro to the vet's surgery and sat anxiously in the waiting room.

The door opened. "Come in! Come and see the patient."

There was Ebony. He was standing on the floor of the cage, a large patch bare of feathers on the side of his neck, and criss-cross stitches closing the wound. He cocked his head and looked at me. He had survived the operation!

"He's had something to eat," said the vet; but there was no food left in his dish. The poor bird must be hungry, I thought, but otherwise he seemed fine. I couldn't stop smiling.

I was told to buy some special disinfectant, dilute it in water and bathe the wound every day for ten days. The stitches would eventually be absorbed and would not need to be removed. Having put his travelling cage back in my bag, I flagged down a taxi as soon as I had left the vet's building. I sat on the back seat with the bag beside me, every now and then opening it at little at the top and making soothing remarks to him. He would tilt his head and look up at me with one round eye, and seemed uneasy, but not

really frightened. Every time the taxi braked, he lost his balance and fell off his perch.

"Have you got a creature in there?" the taxi driver wanted to know.

"It's only a bird."

"Ah – a bird." I think he was worried that some fierce animal might escape into his car. People seldom know what to make of birds.

At last we arrived at my block of flats. I had cleaned out his cage and put in a supply of fresh water, insectivore food and a dish of mealworms. Placing the small cage against the large one, I opened both doors.

Ebony hopped into his home cage with alacrity. He hopped to and fro a few times, puffed up the feathers on his head into a benign rounded shape, whistled sweetly and began at once to gobble his worms.

For several days afterwards he kept this good-humoured appearance and seemed really glad to be home. He didn't even object to the ordeal of having his wound bathed once a day. This I did with the help of Robert, who lived only a short distance away. The operation took two people. One of us would hold him cupped in both hands while the other would dip a sterile compress into the disinfectant diluted in lukewarm water, and squeeze it gently on to his neck. He would breathe rather hard as we were doing this, but didn't utter a sound. Yet on other occasions, whenever we had to handle him to trim his claws, which was necessary as they didn't get worn down as a wild blackbird's would have done, he screamed protests in a voice like a seagull. Now, though, he seemed to realize that we were trying to help him. Sure enough, thanks to this excellent vet, he made a full recovery. He didn't scratch the wound, it healed cleanly and the feathers grew again.

How could I tell that he was happy and in a good mood? It's not difficult to read a blackbird's body language. When he was feeling docile and friendly, his head would be round, with the crown feathers raised and his other feathers slightly puffed out. His eye looked mild and he would make sweet-sounding little remarks, rather like "Pew-pew". When he was in a bad mood, however, his head would be flat and snake-like, his beak pointing forwards and upwards aggressively and all his feathers flattened tight to his body. Sometimes he would open his beak slightly and give a faint, high-pitched whistle: "Seee!"

Blackbirds tend to be rather irascible. When I went into the room in the mornings and approached his cage, Ebony would seem to say to himself: "Let's see: what kind of mood am I in?" Depending on the answer, either his head feathers would rise and he would greet me sweetly, or they would flatten and he would aim a fierce peck at the bars of the cage. There seemed to be no particular reason for his being in a good or a bad temper.

When out of his cage, he seemed positively to enjoy a mock fight. He would be hopping around on the floor. I would sit down, place one hand on the floor and waggle two fingers up and down. "Want a fight?" I would say. This was definitely an aggressive challenge for Ebony, and he would rush towards my hand, beak open and wings outstretched, and attack my hand. I would retaliate by tapping him with one finger and he would dodge back and then return to peck me.

For some reason, he was always in a good mood if I came home late in the evening, when it was already dark in the room where his cage stood. I would turn on the light in the passage and Ebony would great me with enthusiastic "pew-pews" and hoppings from perch to perch, crown feathers raised. He would keep this up while I was cleaning my teeth and preparing for bed with the bathroom door ajar.

"Ebony, you should be roosting."

"Pew-*pew*!"

"Ebony, aren't you sleepy?"

"Pew-pew-*pew!*"

Only when I had wished him goodnight and turned out all the lights would he subside, put his head under his wing and go to sleep.

If anyone else entered the room while it was still dark however, he would be very alarmed. Michel in those days used to keep his shirts in the chest of drawers on which Ebony's cage was standing, and on winter mornings he would sometimes go in and pull open a drawer. Panic! "Pop-pop-pop!" shouted Ebony, falling off his perch. "This bird is so nervous," grumbled Michel. A drawer opening and a shirt being pulled out in the half-light was something very scary, apparently.

The door to his room was usually left open, but when spring came I had to keep it closed at night or risk being woken at a very early hour by loud singing. It was after the end of his first year with me that he started to sing properly. After losing his juvenile feathers, he had begun to make little tuning-up noises, known to ornithologists as subsong, with his beak closed. He sounded rather like a kettle starting to boil. Blackbirds do this on sunny days in the winter, almost as if they are humming to themselves, but you have to be nearby to hear them. In mid-January, when he was about eighteen months old, he opened his beak and started to pour out the full-throated song of an adult blackbird. This rich, rounded whistling and warbling is familiar to everyone, country and town dwellers alike, and is so much a part of spring and early summer that it would be hard to imagine those seasons without it. Although it's recognizably a blackbird's song, each blackbird has a slightly different repertoire, and throughout a season you can recognize the signature tune of a particular blackbird. Sometimes, sitting at my office desk towards the end of a dreary winter afternoon in January, I would hear a blackbird singing loudly in the distance, inspired by slightly milder weather and the light from a streetlamp, and I would feel that spring must be coming soon. Ebony was also influenced by the light mornings in spring, but funnily enough the sound of the vacuum cleaner similarly inspired him: a domesticated bird.

"That dratted blackbird!" complained my friend Karim, who lived in a block of flats in the north of Paris. But he was not talking about Ebony. "Every morning at five o'clock he starts, right outside my window, long before the alarm clock. It's all very well for him – he doesn't have to go to work."

Blackbirds choose a high perch for singing, a topmost branch or the highest corner of a building, and the song echoes across the rooftops, especially in the early mornings and the evenings. In the city, they are the main vocalists in the dawn chorus, which otherwise would consist mainly of the twittering of sparrows or the bubbling moans of pigeons. I feel we city-dwellers are very lucky that blackbirds have

proved so adaptable that they live side by side with us even in the midst of traffic and dense concrete buildings. It's true – they are very loud. However, they all stop singing towards the end of July, and so did Ebony, even though he was living in an artificial environment. In the summer, they moult and don't draw attention to themselves in their scruffy and somewhat weakened condition.

Ebony's repertoire of musical phrases varied and developed as the years passed, and he also imitated other sounds. Car-alarms would often go off in the street for no apparent reason, and Ebony enthusiastically mimicked their two-note "call" in the middle of other warblings. I managed to record his voice, not without difficulty. By the time I had rigged up a microphone and a cassette recorder, he would obstinately decide to spend his time silently preening, eating or dozing. When he did began to sing, I had to creep discreetly forward and switch on without drawing attention to myself.

On returning home from work, I would give an interrogative whistle on a rising note as I opened the front door, and from the other end of the flat he would give the same whistle. As I moved around, unloading shopping and looking at mail, we would whistle to each other: "Phweee? Phweee?" at regular intervals. This had replaced the old "cuckoo" greeting.

If I went into his room, he would alternate his "phwee?" call with "pop-pop! pip! pip!", accompanied by tail-jerking and wing-flicking. These movements may be a sign of aggressiveness, but are often just the expression of excitement. Sometimes he would then start "patrolling" up and down his perch. With head lowered and tail slightly fanned, he would run to one end of the perch, raise his beak, flick his wings and whistle "phwee?". Then he would do the same thing in the other direction. Sometimes I would imitate him, making little runs parallel to his cage and jerking my elbows as I whistled. I dare say I looked odd (well, quite mad, probably) but nobody except Ebony could see me, and he seemed to know what I meant. I think we were both patrolling the limits of our territory, the way two dogs will run barking along either side of a fence.

His cage was definitely his territory. He sang when he was inside it, but I never heard him sing properly, apart from the *sotto voce* subsong, when he was outside it.

How did he perceive me? Certainly at the beginning I was the next best thing to his mother or father – possibly his father, as the males often continue to feed fledglings after the females have stopped because they are busy laying a fresh clutch of eggs. Blackbirds can have several broods in a season, and Ebony must himself have been a fledgling from a late brood, as it was July when I rescued him. Once the female is sitting, the male spends a lot of time singing.

This is certainly not for the purpose of attracting a mate, as he has one already. It's quite probably intended to warn other blackbirds off his territory, as it will be needed for the food supply of the nestlings once they are hatched. When the young are in the nest, there is less time for singing as both the male and the female are kept busy, feeding them on worms and grubs. Young blackbirds continue to beg frantically for food even when, having left the nest, they have learnt to pick things up in their beaks and feed themselves; but gradually this behaviour changes and they become independent. Do they still recognize their parents, or do they see them merely as rivals? We don't know. What we do know is that blackbirds recognize their own young fledglings and seldom or never feed those of other blackbirds, even though to us their plumage and calls are indistinguishable.

No doubt Ebony as an adult saw me as a possible rival with a territory bordering on his own. More poignantly, though, he sometimes viewed me as a possible mate, and would perform a courtship display in front of me. This very distinctive posture makes a male blackbird look quite different from usual, and rather odd, with his crown feathers sticking straight up, his neck feathers flattened, his rump feathers raised between drooping wings, and his tail fanned and lowered to sweep the perch. Looking like this, Ebony would take a mincing run along the perch, uttering a half-choked, beseeching call aimed at me – for want of a real female. When he did this, I would regret that I couldn't provide him with a mate. But that would have been impossible, for a number of reasons. Blackbirds live peaceably in pairs only during the breeding season. At other times, each individual fiercely defends his or her territory, which may be several hundred yards across, and both males and females don't hesitate to fight any intruder that resists being chased away. A small flat with two blackbirds in captivity would have been a war zone.

So by saving his life I had deprived him of mating and breeding. But disabled as he was, with a drooping wing, deformed foot and, above all, a damaged eye, he would almost certainly not have survived to mate and breed in any

case. Nature being ruthless, weaklings are very quickly taken by predators. Among the young, mortality rates are as high as 50 per cent. Nature cares about the survival of the species, not about individuals, whereas we human beings have a different outlook. Some of us have, at any rate. I, at least, certainly couldn't help seeing him as an individual, unlike any other.

Whatever his perception of me, he certainly recognized me, and didn't like it if I went away for any length of time. Sometimes I had to travel abroad to translate documents at conferences, and sometimes, of course, I went on holiday or on short trips to England to visit my family. Various arrangements had to be made for Ebony and the other birds to be looked after during my absence. Some friends took this in their stride, but others were squeamish about mealworms. I remember coming home from a trip and eagerly asking one friend how my birds were. "Full of worms," she replied with distaste. This was the downside of any offer to spend a free couple of weeks in my Paris flat.

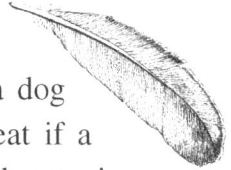

Ebony did not pine when I was away, as a dog might have done, although he didn't like to eat if a stranger was watching him and would adopt a threatening attitude until their back was turned. When I came home, on the other hand, he would be distinctly unenthusiastic at seeing me and would sulk for several days, refusing to whistle back at me and being generally unresponsive.

If it happened to be autumn when he was sulking, I could usually get him to relent by making him a present of some dead leaves. He loved these, immediately picking them up in his beak and bashing them on the floor until they fell to bits. Blackbirds instinctively search for food among leaf litter, turning over leaves with a quick flick of the head and simultaneously scratching the ground with one foot. If you are out walking in woodland, you sometimes get the impression that there is quite a large animal moving about in the undergrowth. Look closer, and it turns out to be a blackbird turning over dead leaves. Even if no grubs were lurking underneath them, Ebony seemed thoroughly to enjoy tossing them about.

Once, Michel and I had been away on a trip and Robert had agreed to come in every day to feed all the birds, collect the mail and generally oversee the place.

We arrived back at the flat early one morning, though later than planned as our flight had been delayed. We were weary and jetlagged. As we stepped out of the lift and I approached the door with my key ready, I stopped dead. "There's a hole in the door. It looks as if it's been drilled." We stared at each other. Burglars must have got in. Perhaps they were still inside.

The door wasn't locked. Gingerly I pushed it open. Would we see a scene of devastation? There was the hall table with the parchment-shaded lamp in the corner. There were the bookcases and the carpet. I couldn't see anything out of the ordinary. What had happened? Then, with a flood of relief, I heard Ebony's signature-tune coming from the other end of the flat. He was all right! No serious harm could have been done if Ebony was all right.

It turned out that burglars had indeed tried to break in, but hadn't succeeded in forcing the lock. They had managed to jam it, though, so that poor Robert had found that he couldn't get in to feed the birds. He had been obliged to call a locksmith, who had managed to open the door, but after that there was no way of locking it again. Robert had in fact been dozing on the sofa as he waited for us to return, but since we were late, he had finally given up and gone home to feed his cats, hoping that we wouldn't be long. After that experience, I paid for a steel door with reliable locks. Nobody was going to break in and hurt my Ebony, at any rate.

One day, Robert came in to find Ebony's cage splashed and streaked with crimson as if there had been a bloodbath.

"What's been happening here?" he asked in alarm.

"Ebony ate a strawberry," I explained.

Some birds eat neatly, holding down their food with one foot. Parrots and Japanese nightingales do this, but many birds have a much messier technique, jabbing at the food, tapping it vigorously on the ground and tossing it into the air. Ebony was definitely one of the latter. Song thrushes, which belong to the same family as blackbirds, have cleverly learned to tap snails on stones so as to smash the shell. A crafty blackbird, while unable to do this himself, will sometimes sneak up, drive away the thrush and eat the ready-prepared snail.

Ebony was a part of my life for such a long time. Life in Paris: the changing light of spring, summer, autumn and winter. Métro strikes. Crises in the office. I had my ups and downs, like everyone else. Sometimes I would come home feeling bruised and miserable, after a conflict at work or a quarrel with somebody. Human beings and organizations can be unbearably complicated. But even if I was embroiled in rows or depressed by disappointments, I felt, whenever I opened my front door, that Ebony was there, that he needed me quite simply and that we accepted each other. It was comforting.

Eventually my long relationship with Michel came to an end, and we split up, though I'm glad to say that we have remained firm friends ever since. To cut a long story short, I had met Jean-Luc (whom I was later to marry), and after a few months he moved into the flat. Ebony eyed him with suspicion, but not outright hostility.

"What is it, then? Are you afraid of me?" Jean-Luc asked him, looking at him through the bars of the cage and doing his best to make friends.

"Pop! Pop!" said Ebony uneasily, flicking his tail.

Jean-Luc had one great merit, at least: he didn't keep his shirts in the drawer under the cage.

The years passed, and I was beginning to feel that I had lived in the city for long enough. As the flat was on the eleventh floor, we certainly had a fairly unobstructed view, but it was still a view across miles of roofs, windows, blocks of flats, chimneys and television aerials. Virtually the only greenery to be seen was the horse chestnut tree in the yard just opposite the bird room. Every spring it burst into a mass of exuberant blossom like cone-shaped candles. Apart from Ebony's singing, it was the only genuine sign of spring. In the city, the weather varies but you don't really see the seasons changing. I used to be glad to watch that tree coming into leaf, forming a green dome in summer and turning brown and gold in the autumn.

Then, one spring day when it was in full bloom, some men came and chopped it down. Yet another block of flats was soon being built on the site.

Jean-Luc and I were already beginning to feel that the flat was too small for the two of us and all our stuff, and for me the tree-felling incident clinched it.

"Shall we look for a place outside Paris?" I thought nostalgically of woods and fields.

"Why not? We definitely need more space." It's a rule of life that stuff expands to fill more than the space available.

So we started house-hunting.

It was all very well to yearn to live in the country, but it would mean the upheaval of another removal, and it would mean moving the birds all over again. How would we manage? Ebony was now an elderly bird. His right eye, the one damaged by the cat, had always had a white streak of scar tissue across it, interfering with his sight on that side. But now he began to get a cataract in his other eye, and couldn't see very well where he was going when I let him out of his cage. Little by little, he stopped flying up to perch on furniture and spent most of his time hopping around on the floor. Since I always put his food and water in the same positions on the floor, and he knew where to find them, he still seemed to enjoy these outings.

When he was in his cage, he would sometimes try to stand on one leg as he used to do in the past, but his feet had grown knobbly and, I suppose, arthritic, and he had trouble balancing on his perch. Once I watched him as he stood on one leg and lifted the other foot. Then he put it down. Then he lifted it again. He put it down. Then he lifted it, began to scratch his head – overbalanced and landed with a thump on the floor of the cage. This didn't seem to bother him. Sometimes he would be singing when he overbalanced, but would continue almost without interruption when he found himself on the floor.

Well, we found our house in the country: an old house, covered in Virginia creeper. It had oak beams and square-paned casement windows with green shutters, and a long garden with rose bushes, a big walnut tree and apple trees. It stood almost on the edge of the forest. Green, growing things, space and fresh air! The scent of the country air in the early mornings and after dark brought back memories of my childhood. Compared with the cramped quarters, noise and pollution of life in Paris, it was like a dream. We decided to buy it.

And so once again I was busy stowing books into cardboard boxes for the removal men, and once again we had the problem of moving the birds. This time we rented a van, in which we planned to transport the bird cages, the plants, my large ornamental weeping fig, and our small supply of wine and whisky. Robert, who also wanted to leave his tiny studio and unsatisfactory part-time job, was moving out of town to live almost nextdoor, and we were taking him and his two cats in the same vehicle.

I shan't, in a hurry, forget that January day when we tried to stuff everything into the van.

"It won't all go in."

"Yes, it will."

"It won't! Why ever didn't you choose a larger model?"

Jean-Luc and Robert wrestled with the thrashing branches of the weeping fig, I worried that the birds in their travelling cages might catch cold, plants stood waiting on the pavement and a neighbour stopped to watch and make helpful comments, such as: "The thing to do is to keep calm." At last we had crammed everything in and set off, driving along the motorway with all the contents rattling, the birds toppling off their perches and squawking, and Robert's cats protesting loudly from their baskets. What were we doing? Why hadn't we stayed peacefully in Paris? We must be mad.

I really hate moving house. So many details must be taken care of, and the removal men were boorish, rude and clumsy. Then all our belongings were in piles of boxes and essential items couldn't be found. I can quite believe that moving house is high on the list of stressful life events. But at last we had a house of our own in the country, and what was more, there was a large outbuilding with plenty of space for bookcases.

The first thing to do in our new home was to find suitable places for all the bird cages, and for Ebony in particular. He still had the same cage, this time in the dining room, and could find his food and water which we always put in the same places, but he couldn't see the room itself. He was very nearly blind, and the gold rings around his eyes were crinkled with age. When we had at last finished

unpacking boxes and getting ourselves organized, I tried letting him out, but he was completely lost. He didn't know where he was, and hopped around in circles, bumping into the furniture. When I put him back in his cage, he seemed relieved.

In the wild, birds don't grow old. According to an interesting book written in the 1950s, and long out of print, *A Study of Blackbirds* by D. W. Snow, only one in 100 blackbirds will live as long as ten years. In captivity, although they have been known to live to be nearly twenty, they can suffer from all the ailments and disabilities of old age. Ebony had lost his sight, he didn't fly any more, and he no longer sang. His feathers looked untidy, as he couldn't balance well enough on his feet to twist and turn and spread his wings and tail in order to preen them. He would try to preen, however, pecking and sleeking his breast feathers. He no longer took complete baths, probably feeling unsure of the depth of the water in front of him, but he would, so to speak, wash his face, and flick drops of water about. He knew when there was a dish of worms in its usual place, and would stab here and there in it until he could grab a worm, and usually managed to eat them all. In the last year of his life, he suffered from an irritation of both eyes. He would rub them on the floor and make them dirty, and every day we had to bathe his eyes, a process that he endured patiently, just as he had when his neck was injured: as if he knew that we were doing it for his good. Robert became practically his nursemaid during the long days when Jean-Luc and I were at work in Paris.

He spent a lot of time dozing, but would peck the bars of his cage with something of his old aggressiveness if he felt someone approach, and he would lift his head and listen if we spoke to him.

Living so far out of Paris, we now had to get up very early and catch the bus shortly after 7 o'clock, then the train and then the métro, if we were to be in time for work. One morning in July, I had breakfast as usual, and went over to Ebony's cage to say hello to him before I left. He raised his head and listened as I talked to him as usual, calling him "little Ebony".

Later that morning, Robert phoned my office.

Ebony had died peacefully, without a struggle. He was sixteen years old. Sixteen long years had passed since that day, also in July, when I had rescued him from a cat.

Now he is buried at the bottom of our garden. I know exactly where, because I had a little tombstone engraved with his dates. The man in the funeral director's office looked at me strangely when I asked for the inscription "Ebony. The lovely bird", but I didn't care. To me, he was a lovely bird, and why should he not have a tombstone?

Since then, we have seen plenty of blackbirds in the garden, chasing one another on the lawn and foraging for food, but they won't come near us. We belong to a dangerous species. Every year there are nests and we hear the loud, insistent begging calls of fledglings hiding in the foliage. One day, one of these flew into the bedroom by mistake, and I had to grasp him where he clung to my dressing-gown on the back of the door. He had tufts of downy feathers on his head, and he screeched, just as Ebony used to do when we trimmed his claws. I took him to the window and opened my hand. Free, he flew across the garden to his mother, who was waiting in a shrub.

On summer evenings, just at dusk, the blackbirds give excited calls: "Pip! Pip! Pip!" and sometimes the chattering shriek of an alarm call. At first I used to check that there was no marauding cat around, but after a while I realized that this behaviour was just part of the excitement of going to roost. Sparrows and starlings also make a lot of noise before they sleep. We don't always understand birds' behaviour, and they certainly don't understand ours.

But Ebony was not just a bird.

For me, he was definitely a person, and I am so lucky to have known him.

PART TWO

SPICA

THE STORY OF A STARLING

J ean-Luc left his office building at a brisk pace. It was early evening in spring, just before nightfall, and he was in a hurry to go to the largest bookshop in Paris and buy some books on software. As he was crossing the footbridge that led along the side of the building and over a car park some fifteen feet below, he passed a colleague.

"Look – there's a little bird," said the colleague.

Jean-Luc glanced down and saw a small fledgling on the footbridge, in imminent danger of falling down among the parked cars, some of which were revving their engines and starting to reverse. The creature had little stumps of feathers and no tail, and was looking up at him with a beady black eye. It clearly couldn't fly, and must have fallen out of a nest somewhere out of sight, high up under the roof of the building. He paused.

"Well, goodnight," said the colleague, and strode off

Jean-Luc hesitated. He needed those software books and didn't want to waste time. On the other hand, this little bird was not going to survive for long where it was. He thought of me. I was at home that evening, in our house fifty miles from Paris, while he was due to spend the night in our pied-à-terre studio flat in the 13th arrondissement. He knew that I had always been a bird-lover, and as a child used to climb trees to inspect nests. I would watch fascinated as parent birds worked busily to raise their young. Our bird table is always a source of food for the garden birds, and I've also owned a number of cage birds over the years: canaries, budgerigars and some more exotic specimens such as Japanese nightingales. Above all, there had been Ebony, the blackbird, whom I had rescued from a cat as a fledgling and who lived with me for sixteen years, singing beautifully every spring until the final years of his life.

If Jean-Luc told me that he had left this fledgling to die, what was I going to say? He whistled softly, and the bird skated towards him on claws and belly, as if answering his call.

There was nothing else for it: he turned round and went back into the office. He dumped a ream of photocopying paper on a desk and emerged again with the empty cardboard box.

I had just finished supper when the phone rang.

"What kind of bird is it?" I asked.

"I don't know. Small. Er… a sparrow? Maybe a blackbird? Anyway, what am I going to do with it?"

"You'll have to feed it."

Jean-Luc had abandoned his shopping plan and taken the foundling back to the studio, where it squatted in its box, still looking up at him quite calmly.

"What with? Breadcrumbs? Milk?"

"No, not dry breadcrumbs, and certainly not milk. Take a couple of biscottes, crumble them up and make a sort of mush with some water," I advised. "Then use a match-stick to poke the food into its beak."

I had had some experience of feeding very young birds, including a sparrow who had gone on to live to the ripe old age of eleven, and I was not about to make the mistake of advising him to give it milk. It always surprises me when people imagine that young birds must drink milk. They are young – but they're not mammals, nor do they drink at all before they leave the nest, as they absorb all the moisture they need from their food. Give a young bird milk and you are likely to kill it. On the contrary, the best food to start with is the kind just described (any kind of dry rusk will do, or wholemeal breadcrumbs at a pinch) mixed with water, maybe a little orange juice, and mashed up hard-boiled egg.

Preparing the mixture is not the only problem, however. The phone rang again.

"He won't open his beak! What shall I *do*?" demanded an exasperated voice.

The thing to do, I explained, is to tap the nest (or box) gently, give a whistle, and make small stabbing movements with the food just above the bird's head. If necessary, tap against the side of its beak. If this doesn't work, it's easier if there are two of you: one to open the beak, a delicate job, and the other to thrust the food down its throat. The swallowing reaction is automatic and the bird usually cottons on quickly and starts begging. But Jean-Luc was on

his own. I wished I could be there, but in the evenings there is no public transport from our village.

Still later the phone rang again and Jean-Luc, sounding rather weary, announced that he had managed to get some food into the little creature.

"But do you think he'll survive if I leave him all night?" He sounded anxious.

With nestlings, the important thing is warmth. Nests are cosy places, and if featherless chicks get chilled during the night, they will die. This had already happened to me. Long ago, I had tried to rear a sparrow nestling. He had no feathers, but took food quite lustily. One evening I came home late and didn't switch on the light to check the nestling before I went to bed. Warm in bed, I didn't realize that the temperature had dropped. Only the next morning did I find the little, naked bird lying in his box, cold and lifeless. I was heartbroken, but it was too late. He was dead, and it was my fault.

"Tear up a lot of paper tissues," I urged. "Put plenty of them around him, and you can even cover him up completely."

"OK." We hung up.

I was looking forward to seeing this bird – *if* he survived until the following day. As it turned out, Jean-Luc continued to feed him until quite late, and then slept fitfully, getting up once in the night to see if he was all right. We had agreed that the next morning he would leave for work as usual. I was to travel in to work on the train, but would make a detour via the studio, collect the bird and take him to the office with me, as he couldn't be left all day without being fed.

When I unlocked the door of the studio next morning, a bowl of mash and a match-stick stood on the table. On the floor in the shower-room there was a cardboard box on its side with white tissues strewn next to it, but no bird. Had he died? Escaped? Then I saw him. He had emerged from his box and had shuffled into a corner, his beak pointing upwards, one liquid black eye observing me. As I approached, he cheeped and opened his beak. This was a good sign.

"Come on, little one," I said. I took a lump of mushy biscotte on the end of the matchstick and whistled. He raised himself up, his open beak like a pinkish orange flower gaping at the end of his swaying neck. Down went the food. "That's right!" He had been a quick learner, and we repeated this operation several times. Then he settled down to digest what he had swallowed. His eyes were half closed.

I remembered my eight-year-old self climbing a tree, and my sense of wonderment at the first sight of the fledglings in a neat heap, beaks resting on scrawny backs, packed into the cup of a blackbird's nest. I had watched the parent birds flying to and fro, first with nesting materials, then with beakfuls of worms. They weren't particularly unobtrusive about it, but I scrambled down from the tree, anxious not to draw any predators' attention to the nest.

Now I stowed the food in my bag, lifted the warm little bird and the tissues into the box, closed the lid and hurried down the stairs to catch the métro to work. No doubt I was the only commuter travelling with such a tiny extra passenger.

A mere thin partition separated my office from the one next to it, and soundproofing was minimal. My colleague poked his head round the door.

"Why do you keep saying 'Open your beak!'?"

"Huh? Well, I – oh, come on, *open your beak!*"

"Oh, I see. You're a mother bird now, are you?" He grinned.

I don't think I got through very much work that day. The bird crouched in his box on my desk, and every quarter of an hour or so I would feed him, trying to keep up the cadence of a parent bird. He had quickly learned to cheep and open his beak, begging for food, but he was still so small, and swayed around as he stretched upwards with beak agape, that it was sometimes difficult not to poke the food into his eye. Between feeds, he either dozed or nonchalantly tried to preen his stumpy beginnings of brownish feathers, while I turned my attention back to paperwork.

A stream of colleagues came into my office to look and comment.

"Isn't he sweet?"

"What are you going to do with him?"

"Are you going to let him go?"

"What kind of bird is he?"

I was already growing fond of him, but the question was indeed what we could do with him – provided that he survived, and at present he showed no sign of enfeeblement. And what sort of bird was he? He didn't look to me like a sparrow, and he certainly was not a blackbird. Judging by the way he seemed to gaze straight up along his pointed beak, he might well be a starling, I thought.

Starlings, living as they do in large and voracious flocks, tend to have a bad press. They roost all together at dusk on city trees and buildings, first of all wheeling, perching,

changing places and making a tremendous din of squawking and chattering. The collective noun for *sturnus vulgaris,* "a murmuration of starlings", must have been coined by someone who heard them at a considerable distance. And of course, many starlings mean a lot of droppings: this is inevitable. On the other hand, they eat vast amounts of grubs and insects that are themselves regarded as pests by farmers and gardeners. City-dwellers suspect them of spreading disease, but studies have shown that they are not serious germ carriers. The fact is that any creatures living together in great numbers tend to be viewed as dispensable, a nuisance, a threat, or little better than inanimate objects. This attitude also extends to people in the mass, if you think about methods of crowd control or the treatment given to asylum seekers or refugees on the move in their thousands. There is something about large numbers which makes us callous. In France, starlings are officially classed as "vermin".

Yet starlings, like house sparrows, are in sharp decline. In the UK, their numbers have dropped from 20 million in the 1970s to fewer than 8.5 million, probably as a result of intensive farming practices and the use of pesticides. What are we doing to our wild neighbours on this earth?

Here, at any rate, was one individual bird, and for me there could be no room for doubt. He was unique, and I wanted to take care of him.

After another phone consultation between our respective offices, Jean-Luc and I decided to take him home with us that evening. Jean-Luc, somewhat bleary-eyed after his broken night, met me in the clattering gloom of the rush hour at the Gare Montparnasse, and we boarded the train. In my bag was the box, and in the box was the bird. The box had a few holes punched in the lid, and I sat with it on my knee in the crowded carriage. "Cheep! Cheep! Cheep!" said the box, audibly and regularly throughout the journey, and people eyed us curiously.

Our house used to be a farm house, and is more than a hundred years old. It has been modernized, but still has old-fashioned terra cotta floor tiles, beams and shutters. To me it feels more real, closer to the earth than the city flat where we used to live, and I've never regretted moving out to the countryside, where you can see the seasons changing.

I put the cheeping box down on the kitchen table and peeped inside. A round eye looked back at me: a Parisian starling was now in a new place. Somewhere in the fir trees at the bottom of the garden, an owl hooted.

"We'd better show him to Robert," I said.

It would have been impossible to keep him at home if Jean-Luc and I had been the only ones to look after him. We were both working full time, and he needed to be fed throughout the day. Luckily Robert, who had become our reliable local handyman, was available. He was already attending to my cage birds and putting out quantities of food every day for the wild birds in the garden,

"Feed him?" said Robert, shuffling in, his woolly hat pulled down over his shaggy hair. He peered at the baby bird, his beard thrust forward. "Feed him? I do everything else around here, so why shouldn't I feed him as well, *hein*?"

Robert's gruffness with human beings disguises a genuine fondness for birds and animals. He did the feeding during the day, and I took over in the evenings and at weekends.

I'm not a very maternal person. Human babies, scarlet-faced and bawling, don't usually fill me with tender feelings. But I've always found that the "Cheep! Cheep!" of such a tiny, fragile creature as a baby bird can't be ignored. People find this a bit odd. Of course, they think, I ought to have stronger feelings for the young of my own species; but the fact is that I don't. I, in turn, find it very odd that some people are afraid of birds and are alarmed by their movements. Hitchcock may have a lot to answer for here. We behave as if there were a gulf between ourselves and animals, and yet we are all on a continuous spectrum of life, and they are our neighbours on this planet.

We moved him into the dining room and kept the door shut, in case either of Robert's cats should wander into the house.

A bigger, deeper cardboard box was found, and I dug out a feeding implement that had already been put to good use with sparrows and my blackbird: a small metal implement like a miniature spade that had come from a manicure set and was intended for pushing back cuticles. This was much less fragile than a matchstick and could be pushed into his gullet without fear of splinters. He adjusted to this quickly and his begging call developed from "cheep" to a more guttural "Churr! Churr!". Nor did he stay for very long in the bottom of the box. Within days, it seemed, he was hopping on to my hand, then scrambling up my arm to my shoulder and even hopping on to my head. Robert, a wearer of woolly hats both indoors and out, could often be seen attending to the cage birds in the dining room with a starling perched on top of his hat, tugging at the wool.

Sometimes, when standing on Jean-Luc's warm hand, this bird would sink down and settle as if on a nest and start to snooze. He had no fear of us whatsoever. We were like giants to this newcomer, and yet he trusted us to keep him alive.

"Do you think we'll be able to release him?" asked Jean-Luc, as he sat at the table with the drowsy fledgling. "Is it fair to keep a wild bird?"

But there could be no question of releasing him into the wild. He had bonded with us now, and wouldn't survive out there, as he had no idea of what was dangerous or what was a predator. Cats were plentiful in the village, not to mention Robert's two, tabby Juju and black-and-white Bidoune. So we had saved his life, but our responsibility didn't end there.

Life with a starling had begun.

"What shall we call him?" we wondered.

The origin of the word "starling" is obscure. Some claim that it was originally "stare-ling", because of the bird's beady gaze. Others say that it was "starveling", owing to its voracity. It certainly has nothing to do with stars, but I couldn't help the star association sticking in my mind. One evening I wandered over to the outbuilding where all our books are stacked on shelves. Pale moonlight filtered through its high windows as I stood leafing through a book on astronomy. Stars and more stars, far beyond the moon. Altair? Arcturus? Polaris? Mintaka?… Spica! How about that? It was the name of a star, but also the Latin for an ear of wheat, and somehow it suggested his somewhat spiky appearance, with pointed beak and apparent crew-cut when he raised the feathers on the top of his head.

Spica it was. Spee-kah.

He had now begun not only perching on the edge of his box, but jumping out on to the table. This was all very fine, but it was hardly practical to have a starling at liberty in the dining room at all times. Our next move was therefore to drive to the nearest pet supplier and buy as large a cage as possible. The dining room already contained other cages, but their occupants lived in them permanently; they were already adult when I had acquired them and so were not particularly tame or used to flying around the room. Spica's cage contained several perches, a swing, feeding dishes, a water pot and some little mirrors on chains, sold as budgie toys. With sand sheets on the floor, it was a well-appointed residence - but clearly we were not going to keep him permanently cooped up in a cage. He liked to be out in the room with us.

It's uniquely satisfying to feel the small weight of a bird on one's hand or wrist. I remember as a child feeding the birds in Bournemouth Pleasure Gardens. They had become so tame, thanks to the efforts of some elderly ladies, that they would fly down to eat broken-up cashew nuts from the palms of our hands. The feeling of their warm dry feet and delicate claws on my skin, for a few seconds each time, was almost magical. The sparrows in London's St James's Park used to be equally tame, but now, alas, there are no sparrows to be seen there. They have all disappeared. Changes in architecture that leave them no holes for nesting? Ruthless farming methods? Nobody yet knows why they have gone. In Paris, although their numbers are declining, they are still around.

By now, Spica's juvenile feathers had grown and he was a greyish-brown colour all over, apart from a darker streak from each eye to the top of his beak. The beak itself still had babyish yellow folds at the corners, giving him a good wide gape for feeding

purposes, and on the top of his head were two tufts of down, like ears. He was endlessly curious, investigating everything and examining things first with one eye, then with the other. When we sat at the table having a meal, he hurried to and fro peering at plates, glasses, bottles and cutlery and tapping everything with his beak (just as babies put things in their mouths) making guttural comments all the time. He walked energetically with a slightly rolling gait, his feet quite wide apart, changing direction frequently, and only bouncing along on two feet if he was in a hurry. Without hesitation he would hop on to my wrist or arm, sometimes pecking my hand or my sleeve. "What's this? What's this?" he seemed to be saying.

He couldn't yet feed himself, however. A bowl of starling food with the cuticle-pusher had to be always available. I had now added some insectivore mix to this, to give him the necessary animal protein. (I have also seen dog-food recommended for young starlings, but haven't tried it.) He would perch on my left wrist and I would feed him, whistling and holding the food just above him, whereupon he would open his beak with louder and louder "churr! churr!" noises, I would thrust the food in, and down it would go with energetic swallowing movements.

He learned to drink before learning to feed himself. Nobody taught him, but after a while he seemed to realize that he should dip his beak into water and tilt his head back so that it ran down his throat. Most birds drink in this way, but not pigeons: they lean forward and suck up the water as if through a straw.

Spica greatly enjoyed perching on my hand and drinking water from my glass, especially as it was chilled water from the fridge. However, his enthusiasm would get the better of him and he would then try in vain to climb into the glass and have a bath, flicking drops of water to and fro and crossly pecking the rim of the glass because it was too small for him.

People often think that parent birds teach their young what to do, but in reality a lot of behaviour is instinctive. There was no way that Jean-Luc or I could teach him to fly. "Are you going to try jumping off chairs and flapping your arms? Ho! Ho!" Our friends thought this was funny. We needn't have worried. When he was fully fledged, he instinctively began flapping his wings, and eventually he took off. He made short practice flights at first, and there were some crash landings, but very soon he had mastered the art and thought nothing of circling rapidly around the room above our heads, shouting raucously.

Soon, he also grasped the technique of feeding himself, but he has never liked anything sticking to his beak or making it greasy, and always wipes it vigorously to and fro on whatever is underfoot, often the nearest person's sleeve.

Jean-Luc had some mustard on the side of his plate, and Spica spotted it. "You won't like it." Too late! Spica had already dipped his beak into the yellow blob. He immediately flew back into his cage and spent several minutes continuously wiping his beak on the perch. That was the first and last time that he tried mustard.

Right from the start he had shown signs of wanting to preen his feathers, and this he now did conscientiously. All healthy birds spend a lot of time every day making sure that their feathers are in perfect order, oiled from a small gland above the tail and so neatly arranged that they form layers that are both warm and waterproof. It's a sure sign that a bird is ill if it has stopped preening.

Spica also knew, without being taught, that baths are excellent for keeping feathers in good condition. After taking some involuntary showers when he tried to climb into the glass I was drinking from, I provided him with a plastic bird-bath and he didn't hesitate to use it. Having a bath seemed to be an exciting occasion. He would walk quickly to and fro beside it, hop on to the edge, take a sip, walk about a bit more, jump in, give a quick flick of his wings, jump out and run his beak through his feathers, walk about some more, jump in and then splash very enthusiastically, alternately dipping his head and his tail, his wings meanwhile sending droplets of water flying in all directions. When he had finished, there would be a pool

of water on the floor, and he would fly in a rather heavy and waterlogged fashion to a safe perch, where a vigorous preening session began, with beak wiped, feathers shaken out, raised and flattened, wings beating in quick vibration, tail wagging from side to side. Head-scratching was also part of this routine, and again, he knew instinctively how to do this, standing on one leg, passing the other foot behind his wing and turning his head at various angles to the rapid blur of his claws. He would give himself a little shake after scratching his head, as if to say "That was nice." At first he used to scratch his head with his beak closed, but in later years he would stretch his head upwards with his beak wide open and then scratch. This was apparently more satisfying. It's interesting that not all birds perform this action in the same way. Pigeons and parrots, for instance, raise one foot in front of their wing, not behind it.

Starlings don't take dust-baths, as sparrows do, but they like sunbathing. When sunlight pours through the window, Spica can often be seen strategically placed with his wings outstretched, his tail feathers fanned, all his other feathers slightly puffed out like miniature cockle shells, his beak agape and his eyes nearly closed, blissfully allowing the warm sunlight to reach his skin.

One piece of starling-like behaviour that distinguished him from young sparrows or blackbirds was the use he made, from an early age, of his beak. If something was lying flat on the table – a mat, for example – he would poke his beak underneath it and try to lift it by opening his strong jaws. Any hole would be explored in the same way, with an attempt to force the edges apart.

"Ouch!" Jean-Luc yelped. Spica had perched on his shoulder and was poking his beak into his ear, trying to enlarge the orifice.

Similarly, he would fearlessly try to prise our lips apart. I couldn't help smiling at his antics, and he was immediately fascinated by the sight of my teeth. He inspected them, first with one eye, then with the other. Then he pushed his head forward and – *tock*! – gave the teeth a quick tap. Everything was strange and interesting to him. Having a beak poked into one's eye was not appreciated, however, and he soon learned not to do this. Nor did we welcome having him land suddenly on our heads and deposit a dropping in our hair.

It's impossible to toilet-train starlings. They have a very quick metabolism and, in consequence, eat often, throughout the day, expelling waste spontaneously and frequently. In other words, they make a lot of mess. Although Spica has a cage, he treats this as his roost and refuge, but the whole dining room is his territory in the daytime. Our wooden table quickly acquired a heavy plastic cloth. Old tea-towels protected the backs of chairs. Newspapers adorned the floor under his favourite perching places. As for Jean-Luc and me, we very soon started putting on blue overalls before sitting down for a meal, and sat there looking rather like delivery workers or cleaners.

"All this for a bird," grumbled Jean-Luc.

"Well, who rescued him in the first place?"

"Shouldn't I have done?"

"Of course you should. You couldn't just leave him there to die. could you?"

"Hmm, well... I suppose he would have died. But I do like to eat in peace, in a civilized manner!"

We often had exchanges like this.

Spica hurried across the table and peered at Jean-Luc's plate. Jean-Luc glared at him, then took a fragment of meat and gently held it out, waiting patiently while Spica eyed it, wondering whether it was dangerous. Then he took it, wiping it to and fro and tapping it on the table to break it into smaller pieces that were easier to swallow. Before he had finished it, he apparently forgot about it, and scuttled back towards me. He seemed to have a short attention span. He would start pecking something with great intensity and then get sidetracked, wondering why he could see a reflection in the side of a bottle and what it was. Then he would suddenly find that his wing feathers needed preening. He would march quickly in one direction, then change and hurry another way, without any apparent goal. Often, however, if he had picked up a particularly large lump of food, he would snatch it, turn sharply aside and stalk quickly away with it as if to ensure that no other starling was going to take it from him.

It's funny the way some species of bird live all together in flocks, yet have vigorous tussles over food. I remember, aged about three, standing beside my father and looking out of a window at a sparrow eating a crumb of bread on our flat roof. Several more sparrows flew down, and one of them snatched it from him. "Oh! What a shame!" exclaimed my father, and went to fetch some more crumbs. But this was in fact quite normal behaviour for birds in a flock. I suppose that pushing and shoving and snatching is one way of ensuring that each individual eventually gets a turn.

When Spica was busy with a piece of food or an interesting object, Jean-Luc found it tempting to lean across and try to touch his tail.

"Touched you! One up to me!"

This was hardly ever successful, however, as he was fully aware of any stealthily moving hand and had almost all-round vision, useful for spotting predators. In the summer, flies come into the house and zoom annoyingly around the room. He can see them perfectly well, but unfortunately can't be bothered to try to catch them in mid-air as I have seen sparrows do, performing remarkable aerial acrobatics. No: he stands there with his head bobbing about as the fly zigzags, sometimes giving an irritable squawk as it zips past his open beak. But why bother, when a plentiful supply of food is placed in front of him every day? He has been known, however, to snap up a tiny insect crawling across the table.

Eating with a beak must be rather like trying to pick up small items with tweezers while one hand is tied behind your back. He will peck, wipe, shake his head, throw the food up in the air, chase after it, try again, find it has landed behind him and perform an agile dance with his claws tapping on the table. He reminds me of a footballer, dribbling and avoiding obstacles with nifty footwork. Once he was struggling to eat half a grape, which was slippery, and as he jabbed at it furiously, he pecked his own foot by mistake. The sharp exclamation he gave was no doubt a starling swear-word. Sometimes the food will fly up and soar right off the table on to the floor. He will look perplexed for a moment, hurry to the edge of the table and peer over. Only if it is particularly delicious will he fly down to retrieve it. As often as not, his attention is caught by something else and he will abandon it.

This eating technique was all very well, but runner beans proved too much for Jean-Luc. I didn't know it at first, but they are one of Spica's favourite foods. One evening I had cooked fish and beans, and barely had we sat down at the table when Spica landed on it with a whirr of wings and a thump. Without a moment's hesitation, he grabbed a bean from my plate. It was nearly as long as he was, and he started wiping it to and fro and tapping it on the table to break it up.

Before he had gobbled more than two beakfuls, he noticed that there were plenty more on the plate, possibly nicer than the one he had chosen. He tried another. Jean-Luc watched disapprovingly.

"What's he doing? Why doesn't he just eat it?"

Bits of bean flew up in the air. Then, despite my protests, Spica grabbed another. And another.

A chunk of bean hit Jean-Luc in the eye.

"That does it! I'm going to eat in the other room!" He took his plate and shoved back his chair. After a moment I could hear shouts, explosions and dramatic music. Jean-Luc was having a peaceful meal in front of the television.

I finished eating and so, eventually, did Spica. But by the time he was having a post-prandial nap on his perch, the whole table was flecked and bespattered with green, rather like a Jackson Pollock painting. I thought that I would probably not serve beans again in a hurry. Peas have also become quite popular, and can be rolled across the table, making him look even more like a crew-cut footballer in action. But beans! His excitement is palpable when he sees them, and although he usually waits politely for me to offer him crumbs of bread, manners go out of the window where beans are concerned and he grabs rudely.

Starlings always seem greedy, but I've found that he will not go on eating out of sheer gluttony, as a dog often will if you let it. When he has had enough, he flies back to the perch just outside his cage and won't show any interest in food for a while. Birds can be artificially fattened, but left to themselves they will regulate their intake.

Starlings are quite omnivorous, but they are basically insectivores and are not seed-eaters, their beaks not being designed for cracking seeds. I had already acquired some experience with my blackbird, Ebony, so I knew that I would have to provide a supply of mealworms. At first we had to take a half-hour drive to the pet shop to buy these, but later I found a mail-order supplier that was much more convenient. Mealworms are not, in fact, worms at all, but little grubs which thrive on bran and bread and bits of fruit, turn into larvae, and then emerge as black beetles, which (if you are lucky) will lay eggs that hatch into grubs, and so the cycle continues. You have to be careful to keep them in some kind of steep-sided container. Even so, it's not unusual to find a worm or a beetle that has climbed out and made its way into some inappropriate place in the house. We needed to bear this in mind when entertaining visitors.

"Aaargh! What's this, crawling?"

I run for the dustpan and brush. "Oh, sorry. Just a mealworm. Let me sweep it up."

Robert counts out the morning mealworms with his fingers, but I'm afraid I am more squeamish.

Living as we do in a village on the edge of the forest, we don't receive too many visitors, however. Our Paris friends regard us as bush-dwellers and hesitate to accept invitations. "What? All that way? We might get lost. Why don't we meet in a restaurant in town?" English visitors are more intrepid, crossing the Channel and studying maps in order to reach us. When we do have other people in the house, of course, there can be no question of eating in overalls off a plastic tablecloth. Spica has to be shut in his cage and the dining room is transformed into a more conventional place for the duration. He takes a dim view of this and makes caustic remarks when I begin my preparations. After a while, however, he seems resigned to the situation and lives quietly in his cage. But after the visitors have gone, and I perform the process in reverse, he knows very well what I am doing, and loud comments of "Kwee! Kwee!" greet every cloth I place on a chair and every newspaper I spread on the floor. As soon as I open his cage, he shoots out and usually takes a bath.

On New Year's Eve he also has to stay in his cage, as I try to make the dining room look festive, with proper place settings and red candles. He isn't alarmed by the candle flames, but I wouldn't risk letting him get near them. We always light a log fire in the sitting room on New Year's

Eve, too, and our dog, Voyou, used to be afraid of it. He seemed instinctively afraid of fire, but not Spica, so I know I have to be careful.

Before midnight I clear everything away, and the patient starling can be let out to start the new year in comfort.

"Happy New Year, Spica!"

"Kwee!" The same remark is suitable for many different occasions.

In fine summer weather, we take our meals outside on the terrace. This is a treat for us, but during a long fine spell I find myself starting to feel rather guilty, as Spica so enjoys sharing our meals, but we have to leave him on his own, indoors in the dining room.

His mealworms are served early every morning by Robert. He certainly knows when they are coming, and makes guttural comments, as if to say "hurry up!" Breakfast-time with worms is probably the best moment of his day. He also has a supply of special insectivore mixture, lettuce leaves and chopped apple. I should not like to work out how much I have spent on these foods over the years. Mealworms are nearly as expensive as caviar, and the special insect mix does not come much cheaper. I watch him rather irritably as he flings it untidily around his cage.

Mealworms sometimes escape from the dish and go into hiding under the sand-sheets on the floor of the cage. It then becomes great fun to find them and tweak them out, either by lifting up the sheets or by pecking a hole. Spica has always liked finding food when the task is made difficult in some way. There may be plenty of crumbs lying on the table, but he would rather poke his beak under my hand and prise it up to seize a crumb that happens to be underneath it, or peck a hole in a paper napkin. I always provide a little piece of wholemeal bread for him at mealtimes, and bits of croissant for breakfast on Sundays are a treat: anything slightly fatty is appreciated. I hold the piece of food on one side of my coffee cup so that he has to poke his beak through the handle to get at it. It tastes nicer that way. Similarly, something that I am eating myself must surely be tastier than food lying around on the table. If I put a crumb between my lips, he will perch on my shoulder, his feet beating an eager tattoo as he peers around my cheek until I turn my head and he delicately grabs the crumb.

Jean-Luc doesn't do this, and regards my behaviour as eccentric. "A bit unhygienic, isn't it?" My husband welcomes dirt, messes and stains the way watchdogs welcome intruders, and, if the truth were told, is not very compatible with starlings... At first, Spica used to perch on his arm or shoulder, walking to and fro and exploring the space between his neck and his shirt collar, or separating strands of hair in the hope of finding a juicy insect; but soon it seemed that he began to feel an invisible force-field of disapproval, and nowadays he very seldom does this, preferring to come to me instead. Jean-Luc still wears an overall, though, just in case. He likes him well enough, but there are limits. It's interesting that starlings sometimes perch on cows' backs and remove ticks from their hide. This may partly explain why he is not very scared of familiar human giants. We're just like lumbering cows.

Every week Spica consumes the yolks of two hard-boiled eggs – eggs being ideal bird-food, after all. He also likes bits of meat, including chicken. "You're eating a member of your own species," Jean-Luc pointed out to him as he gobbled unconcernedly. It was all good protein to him. He is also very fond of fish, which he would certainly not find in the wild. There is no accounting for birds' tastes, however: after all, Ebony used to enjoy home-made ginger icecream.

It wasn't long before Spica began his first moult. As a juvenile, he had uniformly brownish-grey feathers, but now he began to lose them and the spiny prickles of new feathers appeared. These developed into the handsome livery of an adult starling, black with white spots, looking particularly smart on his breast, while his back feathers acquired the shiny iridescence that made them gleam purple and green in the sunlight. His head, though, was the last to moult, and for a while his head seemed to belong to a different bird – scruffy and still greyish-brown, balding in places.

Eventually, this duly gave way to proper speckles, with a handsome black line from eye to beak that made him look rather fierce. When my mother came to stay, she looked at him doubtfully as she paused on the threshold of the dining room. "What a long beak! Will he attack me?" she wondered. This appearance was quite misleading, however, and when he lost these black eye-feathers during a subsequent moult, he took on a mild and gentle appearance until they grew again.

Not that he was always mild. If he perched on your wrist and you waggled a thumb or finger at him, he would take exception to this, stretch up to twice his height, standing on tiptoe, as it were, with all his head feathers raised in an aggressive crest like a warrior's helmet, and threaten the offending finger with his beak wide open and his narrow pink tongue quivering. Sometimes he would attack. But he would subside quickly if the finger stopped waggling and would apparently forget all about it at once. Starlings striding about on lawns, jabbing their beaks hurriedly here and there into the grass, often threaten their neighbours with angry squawks and sometimes chase one another away briefly or fly up in the air in a skirmish, but it's the matter of a moment, and they continue to live and feed together in a flock, just as sparrows and many seabirds do.

If he accidentally got his claws stuck between my fingers or in my sleeve, he would also give an outraged squawk and

peck me furiously until released. Then he would forget the incident.

An aggressive blackbird looks very different from an aggressive starling. Ebony in an angry mood would look like a horizontal missile, all feathers on his head flat and his beak pointed forwards. When he and I had mock fights, he clearly enjoyed them. An enraged starling, on the other hand, is a vertical challenger with crown feathers sticking straight up, but action rarely goes beyond one quick peck.

His full adult plumage was very attractive indeed, the spots on his breast like little white downward-pointing arrow-heads, small on his cheeks and throat, larger on his breast. On his head and back the speckles were brown, and his dark wing- and tail-feathers were elegantly outlined in brown. Wild starlings often have yellow beaks, the yellow

colouring allegedly appearing in the breeding season, but Spica's beak was dark from the outset and has never changed colour, perhaps because he is not exposed to sunlight except through glass. We called him "he", but there seemed to be no way of telling whether he was male or female. To our eyes, the two sexes are identical. All we can say is that he has never laid an egg.

It was about this time that he started to sing. Well, perhaps I should say "vocalize". Starlings of both sexes make quite a lot of noise, whistling, wheezing, chattering, squawking and trilling, their beaks pointed skywards and their throats puffed out and bristling. It's impressively loud – though not nearly as loud as motor traffic – when a flock comes in to roost in the city, but it's a cheerful noise in the garden on a fine day in early spring. Spica began to make noticeable whistles and trills, besides his usual hoarse "kwee!" comments. At the time, I had a very old Japanese nightingale called Mikyo, who lived in a cage on his own. He had a distinctive, continuous up and down warble, and Spica learned to imitate this, so that the two birds often seemed to be talking to each other. Since Mikyo's death, Spica seems gradually to have forgotten nightingale language, but he has his own repertoire of trills and whistles, and is particularly inspired to sing when anyone is using the vacuum cleaner. While preening his feathers after a bath, he makes distinctive little croaking noises, perhaps getting rid of any bits of water-logged feather from his throat.

I learned that Mozart had a pet starling, who lived with him for three years and who could sing the theme from his Piano Concerto in G major. I have tried to teach Spica to whistle "Twinkle, twinkle, little star", but he just eyes me speculatively and says nothing. In recent years, since acquiring Internet access at home, I've discovered fascinating facts about starlings who have lived in close contact with human beings and who have learned to talk, producing whole phrases in little squeaky voices. If we had not been away from home so much, working, perhaps we might have spent more time with Spica and perhaps he, too, would have learned to talk. Unfortunately, this didn't happen, although from time to time he does come out with a remark that sounds very much like "*Petit* Spica, tut-tut-tut". At night, when it is time for him to go to roost, I gradually dim the halogen light in the dining room, meanwhile repeating "*Bonne nuit, brave oiseau,*" or "Goodnight, nice bird," as he hops from perch to perch and settles for the night. Often he answers me with a noise like "kor-kwee" which could, I suppose, be his attempt at "*Bonne nuit*".

The correct position for sleeping is this: first, balance on one leg and tuck the other foot under your breast; then turn your head through 90° and bury your beak in your back feathers; then raise one wing slightly so that the pinions cover your eyes. It looks like the most uncomfortable position imaginable, but clearly for birds it is not. In recent years, however, as he has got older, Spica has found it difficult to keep his head turned backwards. While he dozes, it slips out of position. Consequently, he often sleeps bending forwards, with his tail drooping as a counterweight. He is seldom sound asleep, however, and will wake at the slightest sound or movement. When waking from a nap, he will raise himself on his legs and bow, then raise both wings, shake himself and wipe his beak to and fro on his perch, settle all his feathers, wag his tail from side to side once or twice, and then, with one foot extended, spread one wing and fan out his tail in an elegant movement that reveals each individual feather. A bird's wing is a beautiful thing

How far is it possible to communicate with birds? I'm never sure how much he understands. A colleague of mine, however, got fed up with the starlings which always used to nest just above her terrace and make a mess on the paving-stones. She walked outside one spring and wagged an admonitory finger. "Now, just you go and build your nests round the corner!" she told them. To her surprise, they did.

Spica always knows when I want him to go back into his cage and settle down for the night. "Into your cage," I tell him, and from wherever he is in the dining room he will take a short flight, a bouncing run and a quick hop on to the perch inside his cage so that I can turn out the light.

He has regular conversations with Robert. I can hear them both when I am in the kitchen.

"*Alors, Spica, ça va?*"

"Kwurr! Kwee!"

" *Hé!* Are you going to have a bath?"

"Kwurr!"

"*Hé!* You've made a mess on the mantelpiece again, haven't you?"

"Kwurr!"

Living in captivity, Spica doesn't wear down his claws and beak as a wild bird would, and as a result they become overgrown and we are obliged to trim them occasionally. This is not always easy. First catch your starling. Jean-Luc is nervous of handling him in case he hurts him, but Robert would persuade him to return to his cage, perhaps by putting something interesting on the floor of it so that he would go and investigate. Then it would be a matter of catching and holding him firmly, while I would use nail-clippers. The first time we did this, he became paralysed with terror, and when we put him down he sank on to the table and stayed there gasping, his beak open, unable to move.

"Oh, God. What's wrong with him?" We left the room and watched him through the glass door.

I was almost as scared as he was. Was he going to die of fright? Birds do die in this way when caught by predators, even if they are uninjured. In fact birds usually hate being touched or handled, since in the wild only a predator would grasp them in this way.

The minutes passed, and gradually his panting grew less. He closed his beak, swallowed, opened it again. Then he raised himself on his legs and hopped. He shook himself, flew from the table to his perch and was soon himself again. My heart stopped pounding.

Later, although he didn't enjoy the claw-clipping operation, he seemed to know that we were not about to hurt him. He protested loudly, tried to peck us, and curled his feet up tightly, which made it more difficult to get hold of individual claws. But afterwards he would fly up to a perch and preen his disordered feathers, looking rather ruffled and indignant.

However, nowadays he is getting old, and he seems to have become more nervous and fragile. Once again I am worried when we have to trim his claws, as sometimes, unpredictably, he becomes paralytic with fear. But if we leave them, they start to grow in a spiral shape and make walking and perching difficult, so it has to be done. On these occasions, he knows perfectly well why we want him to go back into his cage: so that we can catch him! And he refuses to go in, flying up to the top of the bookcase and looking down with defiant squawks. I have to take him by surprise and shut his cage door when he happens to be already inside.

Other phenomena frighten him, in particular loud noises, strangers, or large objects moving about. When a man came to hang some new curtains, Spica immediately flew to my shoulder and stayed there, trembling, as the lengths of material were shaken out. Sudden alarm calls from birds in the garden cause him to shoot back into his cage for safety. One day a sparrow-hawk dive-bombed outside the window, sending birds scattering in all directions with chattering screeches from the blackbirds, and I suddenly found Spica clinging to the open neck of my shirt with wings outspread, like some kind of feathered fichu. Yet he could never have had direct experience of a hawk.

Another time, there was again something horribly dangerous in the garden, though I have no idea what it was. Spica jumped on to my wrist, but didn't want any food. In a split second, he had hopped down on to my lap. I realized that silence had fallen outside. Not a sparrow chirped. Another second, and Spica was actually inside my unbuttoned overall, sheltering under my arm – something that he had never done before. It was a little while before I could coax him out.

He was also terrified on the day that we had to move all the bird cages out of the dining room so that it could be repainted. He was in his cage with the doors firmly closed, but when Jean-Luc and I picked up the cage and tried to carry it out of the room, he became petrified with fright, flattened on the floor and gasping with open beak. "Stop! Stop! We have to put him down!" Again I was afraid that he wouldn't survive, and we were obliged to stop moving, place the cage gently on the table and talk to him softly and reassuringly until at last he calmed down. Eventually we were able to move the cage, but very slowly. It's hard to tell exactly what he will find extremely alarming.

During the redecorating, our pale peach-coloured plastic tablecloth was damaged by a heavy piece of furniture being placed on it, and I had to buy another one. The catalogue I had used no longer had that colour in stock, so the cloth I ordered turned out to be a rich apricot colour. Spica did not like this at all. He resorted to all kinds of manoeuvres so as not to set foot on it, sometimes nearly overbalancing as he perched on my hand and reached for food. It was several weeks before he was convinced that it was not dangerous. One day, he bravely rested one foot on it for a moment. Nothing frightening happened. Nowadays he marches about on it quite nonchalantly.

How do birds see colours? Australian bower birds choose only blue materials with which to build their astonishing palaces. I believe that Spica can distinguish certain colours, as he will pick out any green speck of vegetables from a rice dish while ignoring red or yellow items. He seems particularly attracted by green food. My friend Dinah made me a present of a pretty, flowery mug with a green handle. Spica was convinced that the handle must be edible and spent a long time pecking at it before he gave it up as bad job.

Real dangers don't necessarily impress him, however.

I used not to like cats, more particularly because of all the destruction they cause to wild birds. It's true that they hunt for fun, even when they are well fed. So do the local

men who go out shooting in the countryside nearby, waking us with gunfire at the weekends during the hunting season, in ominous counterpoint to the crowing of cocks and the tolling of the church bells. They claim it as a traditional right won for commoners at the time of the French Revolution, since previously only the king and the nobility were entitled to hunt. But it seems to me that our thinking about wildlife should have moved on since the eighteenth century, and I belong to an anti-hunting association.

Cats, true enough, are natural hunters. But Robert's tabby, Juju, was such a sweet-natured cat that I really missed her when she died. I suggested to Jean-Luc that we adopt a rescue.

"What? Another animal? No, no, that's not a good idea."

So we did adopt one: a lively one-year-old called Sacha. And he adored Jean-Luc, as most animals do.

The glass-panelled dining room door is usually kept bolted. This was not the case at first, but we knew very well that cats could peer in and watch the birds. We would be sitting at the table and realize that a tabby face was glaring tigerishly through the glass, green eyes focused on every movement. Spica paid no attention to it whatsoever. Then one day we saw Sacha, the tiger in question, jumping up to try the door handle with his paw.

"We'll just have to put a bolt on the door."

"Ask Robert." Jean-Luc sighed. "Whatever else have we got to do to turn this house into a menagerie?" He stumped off to switch on his computer.

Not long afterwards, we came downstairs one morning, and as I was going into the kitchen to make the coffee, I realized that Jean-Luc was staring transfixed at something on the sitting-room floor.

"What's happened here?"

At the alarm in his voice, I went to look. Scattered around on the tiles were brownish feathers. Scenes of slaughter flashed through my mind.

As one person, we dashed to the dining room. What terrible accident had happened? How had a cat got in?

Spica, unharmed on his usual perch, shook himself, flapped his wings, and looked at us with his head on one side. I breathed again.

It turned out that Sacha had caught a sparrow in the garden and brought it into the house. Robert had got rid of the poor victim, but some feathers had been left drifting around.

Since then, all cats have been obliged to wear large jingling bells on their collars. Robert's latest acquisition, Câline, is a very docile ginger female who spends more time in our house than in his, and who sits outside the dining room door miaowing plaintively, as much as to say that she would never, never harm a starling if allowed in. But we don't believe her. Bells notwithstanding, she quite regularly brings live mice into the house, letting us have an interesting time with brooms and a shrimping net as we try to catch them so that we can release them into the garden again.

"You ought to catch mice *inside* the house and take them *out*," Jean-Luc tells her severely. She just purrs.

You might expect that Spica would have tried to fly out of the door if it was left open, but this happened only on two or three occasions, when he was very young and before the arrival of Sacha. Exploring, he flew through the kitchen and into the sitting room, but was wholly disoriented and I found him standing on the shelf of a bookcase like an ornament, panting and panic-stricken. I held out my hand, he stepped on to it and I took him back to the dining room.

Another time he landed on the sitting room floor, and this could have been much more serious. Did I mention that we had also rescued a dog? ("Too many animals! They make the place dirty.") Voyou was a mongrel, brindled, and built like a more powerful version of a German shepherd. He saw Spica land on the floor and his ears flicked upright. Not very old himself, he was keen on catching little creatures. Once he had pounced on – and swallowed – a field mouse before I could stop him, the tail disappearing down his throat.

"NO!" I yelled. The dog hesitated, and I sprang to hold him down by his collar, uttering awful warnings, so that he didn't dare move as I stepped towards the bird. Spica didn't move either, cowering on the floor-tiles, and again I held out my hand to rescue him. That was a near thing.

Nowadays, however, he doesn't attempt to leave his familiar surroundings. He has realized that the unknown can be scary.

Other hazards could include swallowing something inappropriate, such as a bead (which might look like a berry) or a rubber band (which Ebony once mistook for a worm). One day, Spica was standing on my shoulder combing my hair with his beak and pecking at my ear. Jean-Luc and I were having an argument and I was not paying too much attention to the cheeky starling.

"These delinquents on the estates north of Paris, they have to be stopped." Jean-Luc waved his fork. "Limits have to be set. The police – "

"Yes, but how did these guys get to be like that? They've got no jobs, no future, their fathers have often gone missing, they're surrounded by gangs of drug addicts –"

"You always try to find excuses. I know they're deprived, but people still have to take responsibility for their actions!"

"I know they do, but you have to remember – "

"How would you feel if one of them pushed you over and stole your bag? Or set fire to our car? Only last week I saw – "

"Yes, but – "

"I tell you – "

"Hey! HEY!" I jumped up and Jean-Luc looked at me in surprise. Our arguments didn't usually result in my becoming violent.

Suddenly I had felt something being loosened from my ear-lobe. Spica had flown off with my stud earring! If he swallowed it, it might kill him. He flew in a circle over our heads, but as I made a move to grab him, he was startled. He dropped the earring. Phew.

Why had he stolen this sparkling little thing? Just because he could, of course.

Shiny objects were of great fascination when he was younger. He would pick up the tin-foil lid of a yoghurt carton and bang it on the table as if his life depended on it. This is the technique used for breaking bulky food into more manageable pieces, but for a long time he was not discouraged by the fact that the foil lid refused to break. He would also spot his reflection in the concave surface of a spoon and try to fight it.

Breaking things up or pulling them to pieces is fun. We learned this the hard way. At first I had plants on the indoor windowsill, but Spica began to toss clods of earth around and then to pull up the plants by the roots. Plants were banished. At first I had books in the bookcase, but Spica decided that it was entertaining to perch on top of them and rip bits of paper from the pages or the spine, not to mention doing droppings on them. In a procession, Jean-Luc and I spent a whole evening carrying out all the books and replacing them with hard-cased video and audio cassettes. These did not discourage Spica, however, who soon found favourite hidey-holes between the tops of the cassettes and the shelf above. Starlings appreciate holes, and build nests in them. Scrub as we do, and spread newspaper as we may, I'm afraid that the shelves themselves will never be as clean and white as they once were.

"Any other special arrangements to be made for this dratted bird? Hmm? Are you sure?" Jean-Luc sank wearily into a chair.

Being a French starling, Spica is not averse to a drop of wine. In view of his attempts to climb into wine glasses and his tendency to knock them over by perching on the rim, we switched to using tumblers instead. Pouring a glass of white wine is a sure way of encouraging Spica to land on the table. He pecks the outside of the glass and would certainly help himself if I let him. Usually I dip one finger in the wine and allow a couple of drops to trickle down the outside of the glass. He pecks them hastily as they travel downwards and then tries to anoint his feathers with them. Of recent years, however, the feather-anointing has diminished and he actually swallows the drops. Once, when Jean-Luc was away, I had just put my supper on the table and poured half a glass of white wine when the phone rang. As I was answering it, I looked back through the glass door, and there was Spica perching on the glass as boldly as you please and taking repeated sips of wine. I therefore ration him severely. I'm not having a drunken starling flying crookedly around the room.

It seems to be the piquant taste of the alcohol that inspires him. Once, we were eating Vietnamese "nems" that one dips into a little dish of Nuoc Mam sauce. Before we could stop him, Spica was helping himself and spreading drops of sauce all over his wing and tail feathers. "Right," said Jean-Luc resignedly. "I'm not eating any more of this sauce." This odd behaviour seems to be linked to birds' habit of "anting", which involves picking up hapless ants and placing them among their feathers. The alarmed ants secrete formic acid, which is apparently a good conditioner. Nuoc Mam sauce must feel similar, but nems are now off the menu for us.

The years have rolled by. Spica the starling has lived with us for more than ten years. I sit in the cloth-swathed dining room, clad in my overall, eating breakfast from the plastic-clothed table. Spica is on my right shoulder, combing my hair, poking at my neck, and preening his feathers. I can hear the little riffling noises that he makes as he nibbles and sleeks. After a minute or so he sinks lower on my shoulder. I turn my head slightly and can feel the tip of his beak just resting against my cheek. We stay like that for a while.

He has outlived all but two of my other birds, the three cats, Juju, Bidoune and Sacha, and Voyou the dog. It's so sad that most animals' lifespans are much shorter than ours. How will I feel, I wonder, when no one any longer welcomes me with "Kwee!" as I enter the dining room, or croaks "Kor-kwee" as I turn out the light?

My views on captive birds have changed somewhat over the years. Very probably I shall not acquire any more cage birds. I don't think that it is cruel *per se* to keep birds in cages, particularly if they have never known any other life, but I am aware that they lead fuller – if much shorter – lives in the wild. Nor would I ever deliberately take a starling from the wild; indeed, it's illegal to do so in the UK, though not in America. European starlings were deliberately introduced to the United States in 1890, when they were released in New York's Central Park. They have thrived, but as a non-native species they are not protected there. Nor are they protected in France, where they can legally be shot or trapped. Corsicans even turn them into pâté.

The fact remains that the three originally wild birds whom in my lifetime I have known most intimately – a sparrow long ago (successor to the nestling that died), a blackbird and a starling – would all have perished within days or hours if a human being hadn't intervened. Captivity or death? That was the choice. Spica is slightly smaller than the wild starlings I see squabbling around the bird table. Despite all our care and feeding, his muscles have not developed like those of his cousins, and he has never known the experience of flying in a vast, spectacular cloud of others, drifting like smoke and wheeling, turning all at the same time with the flick of a wing. He has never lived in a flock as he should have done. Nor has he been able to mate or breed. To that extent he has been deprived. But starlings are sociable birds, and he has had company all his life in the form of other birds and people.

Sometimes, from a distance, he watches the activity around the bird table just outside the window, where crowds of blue tits, great tits, coal tits, sparrows, dunnocks, chaffinches, greenfinches, blackbirds, the occasional robin and other starlings, too, come to feed. There are even nuthatches, occasionally a beautiful great spotted woodpecker, and in winter a charm – lovely collective noun – of goldfinches, such elegant birds with their red, white and black faces, gold barred wings and polka-dotted wing-tips and tail. "Elegant" is actually part of their official name in French, although their behaviour is anything but elegant. "Tsi-tsi-tsi-tsi-tsi!" I hear, as they chase away the sparrows.

Spica is not as colourful as they are, but I wouldn't exchange him for any more exotic bird. Not I. And he shows no sign of wanting to join any of them.

He has already lived more than twice as long as one of his cousins in the wild. The death rate of the young, particularly of small birds, is very high. In order to survive a freezing winter night, a blue tit, for example, has to eat its body-weight of food during the day, and many do not survive. They need our help. To that extent, Spica has been lucky. He has adjusted to our ways, and we have adjusted to his. And to see him perching on the table, almost touching Jean-Luc's elbow, trilling away, not necessarily interested in food but just wanting to be close to somebody, is to be convinced that he is not unhappy.

As for me, gaining the lasting trust of a living creature of a totally different species has always been a privilege that I will never forget.

First Ebony, my delightful small companion.

Then Spica, who has truly been a little star in our lives.

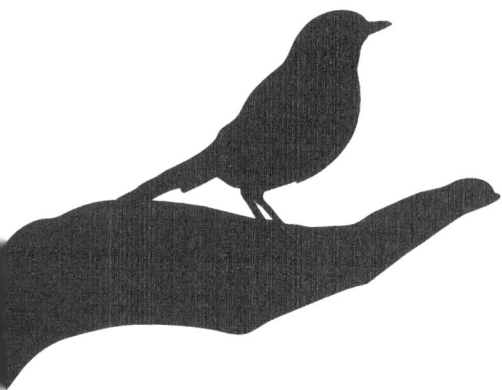

POSTSCRIPT

One morning in July, when I had just finished taking a bath, I again heard a great commotion in the garden, just as I had done so many years ago. Blackbirds were giving a chorus of staccato "Pip! Pip! Pip!" alarm calls, and I hurried downstairs in my dressing gown.

As I crossed the lawn, Robert's latest cat, a large tabby called Figaro, came strolling to meet me. He rolled on his back at my feet, stretching luxuriously.

"What's been going on here?" I asked sternly. The pair of blackbirds were still flying to and fro and hopping agitatedly in the branches of the apple tree.

Figaro rose smoothly to his feet, glided ahead and stopped with his nose pointing to a clump of long grass. I parted the grasses, and there, motionless, was the small speckled shape of a very young blackbird. Figaro sauntered nonchalantly away, as much as to say: "You eat it if you like. I'm not particularly hungry." But I knew Figaro, and quite often a pathetic patch of feathers scattered on the ground would show where he had managed to catch and eat a bird, despite the jingling bell on his collar.

I picked up the little blackbird, who struggled feebly. I looked around for a safe place to put him so that his parents could return to feed him, but I couldn't find a place that was also out of reach of Figaro. I tried to deposit him on a branch of the apple tree, but since he was so young, his claws wouldn't grip the branch. He must have only recently toppled out of his nest. So what could I do? I took him indoors.

Once again, I had a young bird in a cardboard box in the dining room. Spica was at large, sometimes in his cage and sometimes busying himself around the room, but at first he paid no attention to this newcomer. I began to search through the cutlery drawer in the kitchen. Where on earth had I put the little feeding spatula that I had used for Ebony and then for Spica? At last I found it, under a pile of spoons. Once again, I boiled eggs, crushed biscottes and made a suitable mush, only this time I added a handful of insect food. Once again, I began the task of feeding this hungry little bird, who raised himself up, cheeping loudly, and opened a big pinkish orange beak, outlined in yellow, every time he heard me approach his box.

I had various appointments in Paris and couldn't stay at home to look after him all day long, so once again Robert took over, grumbling crossly. When Jean-Luc came home at the weekend, he couldn't resist the urgent demands and also took his turn at feeding.

But there was nothing wrong with this bird. He was fit and healthy, quite uninjured, unlike Ebony. After a week, he was hopping about and trying to jump out of his box, so eventually I gave him the run of the dining room. At first he stayed mainly on the floor, continuing to beg for food, just as Ebony had done, when he was out of reach under the table or underneath a cupboard. I bent and stretched and each time managed to poke food into his wide-open beak.

As the days went by, he explored the room, and then began to jump on to the furniture and finally to fly, as his wing and tail feathers grew. But although he was still speckled, his tail was completely white at the base and black at the tip, while his wings were also flecked with white: quite a natty appearance. Albino blackbirds are not unknown, and it's quite common to see one with just a few white feathers among the black. His head, of course, was still speckled,

so he lacked the gold ring around the eye and his gaze was mild and inquiring. We called him "he", as the French for blackbird is the masculine noun *merle*, but of course "he" may have been a female. I rather think he was a male, though, as he made little remarks to himself as he explored, just as Ebony had done. Females have to be less vocal and more discreet, so as not to attract predators' attention when they are sitting on the nest.

Ebony and Spica had never had a confrontation, but now poor Spica began to discover what a boisterous blackbird was like. When he wasn't pulling vigorously at the cloths that I used to protect the chairs, he was ripping up pieces of the newspaper spread on the floor, and when that palled he would go and bother Spica. He insisted on invading his cage, despite Spica's furious protests, spiky raised feathers and threatening open beak. Within a fortnight, he had grown bigger than Spica, who found himself being chased around the room, especially in the mornings when this blackbird was at his most energetic. In desperation, Spica would take refuge on the floor under the cupboard, but the blackbird would also land on the floor and scoot underneath it too. Desperate squawks of "Kwee!", from *forte* to *fortissimo*, came from under the cupboard, and sometimes I knelt down in alarm to see whether murder was being done. But although they aimed pecks at each other, they apparently didn't hurt each other.

While I was sitting at the table, Spica would perch on my shoulder, where he felt fairly safe. But the blackbird would land fearlessly first on the table, then on the back of my chair, and I would hear an outraged "Kwee!" close to my ear as Spica performed a neat pirouette and tried to warn him off.

By now, the blackbird was preening, taking baths and feeding himself like an adult. He would tear up scraps of newspaper and swallow them. He would pick up and gobble raisins or crumbs of bread if I tossed them to him. But whenever he heard me open the door, he would come flying towards me with a rush of wings, making little "pew-pew" noises, and would still beg to be fed with wide open beak. He would scuttle along the floor near my feet as I walked towards the bowl of food, and I had to be careful not to step on him. After dark, if I had to go into the dining room for any reason, I would hear very soft "pew-pews" coming from somewhere near the ceiling where he had found a perch on which to roost.

I hadn't given him a name. I didn't want him to become so tame that he couldn't survive in the wild, and I didn't want to grow too fond of him. He had reached his adult size and he was healthy and vigorous. Seeing how tame Spica was, he might have come to perch on my wrist or shoulder, but I didn't encourage him.

I had been obliged to remove pictures from the walls, as he now had no problem at all with perching and would land on the top of picture frames, threatening to send them crashing to the floor. Once he landed on the halogen lamp and stood there with his wings outspread, enjoying the heat until a thin plume of smoke began to rise, and he flew off. He had singed his tail!

I knew what I had to do, but it was not easy. There was absolutely no reason to keep him in captivity, and he was making a nuisance of himself to Spica.

He knew all the possible perches in the dining room, and he hopped nonchalantly in and out of Spica's cage all day. If Spica took a bath, he would come and pester him because he also wanted to take one. It was fascinating to watch him exploring, tugging on cloths and newspaper, peering into corners, flying gracefully from one side of the room to the other or taking urgent little runs across the floor tiles or the table. Spica became increasingly irritable, shouting "kwee!" every time the blackbird invaded his personal space, and even shouting "kwee!" at me if I happened to move my arm or hand closer to him when he was standing on the table next to me.

Jean-Luc and I were due to take a trip to England. The blackbird had occupied our dining room throughout August, growing from a small fledgling into a full-sized bird. Although it was touching to see him come flying or hopping to greet me nearly every time I passed in front of the glass door, and although he would still beg for food with open beak and fluttering wings (inspiring Spica to come forward and demand some baby-food at the same time), I had no good reason to keep him in captivity.

It was the day before the journey to England. Jean-Luc was still at work, so Robert and I were left with the task of catching him. This was not easy, and we had to chase him round the room. I hated to see him so frightened of us all of a sudden, when until then he had been so trusting. He kept dodging us, his round eyes bewildered. At last I had to resort to the shrimping net. I grabbed him, he screeched, and I thrust him into a small cage that had once housed a very elderly canary. We left him for a few minutes to calm down: he was panting with open beak. Then I put the cage into a bag and we set off down the village street towards the grounds of the château, where I hoped he would be safe from cats. There were far too many cats in the village itself. I looked into the top of the bag from time to time,

and he peered up at me sideways, just as Ebony had done when I had taken him to the vet. He had no idea what was happening to him.

We passed through the gates of the château, crossed a little bridge over a stream and walked over some rough grass to a clump of trees, beyond which was a broken-down fence and thick vegetation that blended into the forest. I lowered the bag on to the grass and drew out the cage. The great, unfamiliar outdoors was all around him. He screeched again and flapped about, his claws gripping the bars. Talking to him gently for the last time, I opened the door of the cage.

With a rush of wings and the flash of a black and white tail, he immediately swooped into the mass of leaves and branches and vanished.

"We shan't see him again," said Robert.

We stood for a few moments, but there was no further sign of him. Somewhere, we could hear "Pip! Pip! Pip!" but that may have been another blackbird altogether.

A lump came to my throat as I stood there, bereft, holding the empty cage. Then we turned and walked home.

I did miss him. No more glad cries of "pew-pew-pew" met me when I opened the door of the dining room. There was considerably less mess on the floor. Spica, I think, must have breathed a sigh of relief, and he was so exhausted that for the next twenty-four hours he stayed in his cage, resting. But we had surely done the right thing. I could only hope and pray that this unnamed blackbird would manage to live like the wild creature that he was, and that he wouldn't immediately be caught by a hawk or a fox. Would he find enough to eat? Would he find water? It had been a hot, dry summer. How would he cope with bad weather? I would never know.

At least I still had dear old Spica, for a little while.

Eventually, I shall have no more birds in the house. Instead, as a long-time supporter of the RSPB, I shall watch them in the garden as they flit and squabble around the seed and peanut feeders and the food scattered on the bird table:

sparrows and starlings, finches and tits and blackbirds, robins and nuthatches. In spring they will bring their young, who will open their beaks and flutter their wings, and I shall watch them through binoculars.

I simply can't imagine a time when there will be no birds in my life.

THE END

Lightning Source UK Ltd.
Milton Keynes UK
UKOW07f1535301114

242412UK00012B/50/P